BUYING YOUR NEXT CAR

BUYING YOUR NEXT CAR

J. Michel White

WINGS BOOKS

New York • Avenel, New Jersey

About the Author

Michel White has had a passion for cars since he was 15 years old and bought a 1948 Plymouth for $50. It burned more oil than gas, but it was love at first sight and that feeling has never changed. In fact, to date Michel has owned more than 200 cars of all types. Ultimately, his passion for cars found its way into automotive sales and management where he received numerous sales achievement awards from both the dealership and manufacturers.

Dedicated to the memory of
Ivan Millard

This 1995 edition is published by Wings Books,
distributed by Random House Value Publishing, Inc.,
40 Engelhard Avenue, Avenel, New Jersey 07001,
by arrangement with Harbinger House

Random House
New York • Toronto • London • Sydney • Auckland

Printed and bound in the United States of America

8 7 6 5 4 3 2 1

Library of Congress Cataloging–in–Publication Data
White, J. Michel.
Buying your next car : how to stick it to the dealer before the
dealer can stick it to you / J. Michel White.
p.   cm.
Originally published: New ed. Tucson : Harbinger House, 1993.
ISBN 0–517–12412–2 (hardcover)
1. Automobiles—Purchasing. 2. Consumer education.   I. Title.
[TL162.W465   1995]   95–12667
629.222'029'6—dc20   CIP

Contents

Introduction

Thank you! I want to express my sincere appreciation to all of my readers. You have made the first two editions of *Buying Your Next Car* rousing successes, proving that you can beat dealers and sellers at their own game!

A great deal has been happening in the automotive industry since the last edition of *Buying Your Next Car*. Car and truck sales have improved significantly: 1993 new car and truck sales reached almost 11,000,000 units, final 1994 sales figures promise to be even better, and 1995...well, unless there is a severe economic downturn, things look good for another record year. Car and truck prices continue to rise: 1995's **average** domestic prices may finally surpass $18,000.00 and **average** import prices will peak at over $22,000.00.

What does this mean to you, the buyer? It means that deals are still out there, but when the market is good for sellers, they assume what I refer to as a "King Kong" posture, an attitude that says, "We're selling a lot of cars so we don't have to give them away!" This means that in your resolve to see your game plan through from start to finish, you must be tougher, stronger and better educated.

Now more than ever, you must USE THIS BOOK. Dealership sales personnel are continuing to sharpen their skills. Used car sellers, whether dealer or private party, could very well benefit from the dealers' "King Kong" posture, as well, because it has the potential of increasing the demand for, and driving up the value of, used cars.

One of the questions I am asked most frequently is, "When is the best time to buy?" I believe that if you are a thoroughly educated and prepared buyer, any time is the right time. Many feel that the end of the month or the end of the year provide more opportunities for bargains, but this is not necessarily true. Often, dealers actually net more profit at the end of the year because increased factory–to–dealer incentives on close–out models will offset any discount the dealer may give customers. So, don't fall into the month–end or year–end trap. The bottom line is, if you're not prepared, NO TIME IS THE RIGHT TIME. If you are prepared, ANY TIME IS THE RIGHT TIME.

I do not profess this book to be the ultimate source of information, neither do I pretend that I was the world's greatest car salesperson. But I do offer you good, sound advice and common sense techniques to help you—the consumer—get the best car deal possible. This book will do you no good if you toss it on the table and never pay attention to it. Mark it up, make notes in the margins, use the worksheets provided in the back. When you go shopping for your car, take this book with you—and keep it in clear sight when talking with salespeople. I promise they will treat you very differently when they realize you are well prepared, confident and ready to meet them head–to–head.

BUYING YOUR NEXT CAR

To Win the Battle, You Must Have a Plan

The automobile! For almost 100 years, people have been under the enchantment created by this combination of metal, rubber, cloth, and plastic. From the simple single-cylinder engine models with chain drive capable of fewer than ten miles per hour, to the ultimate supercars of the 90s with top speed of more than 200 miles per hour, the automobile has always been and will always be a status symbol. For many people, owning a car is more than just necessity—it is a passion. They cherish the gleam of the paint and chrome, the sweet harmonic sounds of a well-tuned engine, and the exhilarating feel of acceleration. For others, it is no more than a means for getting from one place to another. Each of us has a unique reason for wanting a car—but the bottom line is, at some point almost everyone will buy one. Be it from need or desire, the time will come when you undertake the challenge of going out to buy a car.

That's exactly why you have purchased this book. You are going to buy a car—or at least you are seriously considering buying one. New or used, it doesn't really matter. The thought of actually *buying* a car is something most people truly dread. Most people change vehicles every six years. This means that we participate in something we really dislike, and then don't really give it another thought until we put ourselves through it again six years later. Why do we do this? Why is buying a vehicle so distasteful?

The simple fact is that whether they are considering a new car or a used car, the majority of people genuinely believe they are going to get ripped off when they buy. They perceive that the rip-off will be in the form of either an overblown inflated price that gives the seller thousands of dollars in profit, or a shabby car of inferior quality "dolled up" and patched together to look good and last only until it's driven home. There are valid reasons for these fears and anxieties. The majority of cars sold, whether new or used, are sold by car dealers. On a scale of 1 to 10, 1 being worst and 10 being best, most people rate the honesty of car dealers at 1 or 2. Look at the way car dealers and their salespeople always seem to be portrayed in movies and on television— with loud, flashy clothes, greasy hair, shiny patent-leather shoes, and overbearing personalities, waiting to squeeze every dime out of our pockets. This reputation was not earned overnight, and it will not soon be forgotten.

The era after World War II was a period of tremendous growth in America, especially for car manufacturers and their dealers. Consumers were eager to spend, and dealers were even more eager to take their money. At that time, car manufacturers were not required to use "window stickers" which itemized the car price, and many dealers took advantage of this. They made up their own prices, promising options that weren't there after the customer signed the contract and making claims that could not be substantiated. Dealers got together and fixed prices so that if consumers shopped, they wouldn't find a better deal. There were countless ways a used-car dealer could make a car run well "for a little while." Things finally got so bad that the federal government stepped in. As a result, the Monroney Act was established, which required all manufacturers of cars and trucks sold in the United States to place a "Monroney sticker" on the window of any new car. This sticker must clearly show the manufacturer's suggested retail price of the car plus all factory-installed options and delivery charges. The automobile industry is the only industry that is required by law to place stickers of this type on its products.

This early track record created such mistrust that I don't believe it will ever be fully erased. I am not implying that all dealers are dishonest; on the contrary, there are many fine, reputable dealers out there. But they are in business to make money, and the objective is to make as much money on each and every deal as they possibly can. No matter how they try to change their image, consumers do not believe or trust them.

Another reason for this mistrust is that the average car buyers are totally uneducated about the car-buying process. They take no time to prepare, and they understand nothing about negotiation or how to protect themselves. They wing it.

Buying a car is, in most cases, the second-largest investment you will make in your life (next to owning your own home). How could you possibly consider taking such a step without adequate preparation? You **must** have a **plan of action** in order to undertake and succeed in purchasing a car.

Your bottom-line objective is simple:

- You want the best possible deal you can get on the car you have chosen.

The seller's bottom-line objective is simple, too:

- The seller wants to make the highest possible profit on the car you buy.

We have two direct opposites here—and if you don't have a plan, you lose. *To fail to plan is to plan to fail.*

New-car dealers have a plan, used-car dealers have a plan, even private parties selling their cars have a plan of sorts. Dealerships spend incredible amounts of money training their sales forces to do over and over, each and every day, what you do once every four, five, or six years. Who do you think is going to have the advantage?

Why don't we even up the odds a little bit, and make buying your car not only fun but challenging! I promise you that if you use this book, you can actually look forward to going out and buying your next car!

So, what exactly is your plan of action? This really depends on whether you are buying a new or used car, because the process is not going to be entirely the same. However, basically there are 11 steps involved in buying a car:

Step 1. Determining Your Budget.
Step 2. Determining Your Needs.
Step 3. Understanding the Seller's Plan:
        The Car Dealer's Plan of Action.
        The Private Seller's Plan of Action.
Step 4. Knowing Your Financial Position.
Step 5. Determining Your Trade-in's *Real* Value.
Step 6. Shopping for Your Next Car.
Step 7. Determining the Cost (the Seller's Value).
Step 8. Selecting and Test Driving a Car.
Step 9. Negotiating the Deal *You* Want.
Step 10. Completing the Paperwork (Finance Contracts and Bills of Sale).
Step 11. Taking Delivery.

We will look at each of these steps, as well as these issues:

- Should You Lease?

- Extended Warranties—Are They Worth the Price?

At the back of the book, I've included a complete series of payment tables that relate interest rates to the monthly payment you have budgeted. There also is a Plan-of-Action Workbook at the back to help you organize your strategy. This program and your completed plan of action will give you the single most important thing required in any successful negotiation:

Control!

Your ultimate success will depend upon your ability to take and maintain control from start to finish. By following your plan of action, you *will* maintain control. Maintain control, and you will succeed!

Determining Your Budget

When most people buy a car, first they determine what car they want, and *then* try to fit it into their budget. This is *exactly* the opposite of what should be done if you want to save money and buy the most car possible. Your budget will decide whether you can afford to buy *new* or *used*. It is possible for those of you who *can* afford a new car to want to buy a used car, but it is realistically not possible for those of you who can afford only a used car to buy new. You need to clearly and honestly determine this, and accept the limitations that you establish. To do otherwise and take on more of a burden than you can easily support is not worth the headache and possible financial hardship that will almost certainly arise later, just for the sake of driving a "brand-new" car. If you plan to pay cash for your next car, then you have a predetermined amount at your disposal and your budget may not be drastically affected. But there will be changes to consider, even though you may not have a car-loan payment.

What is your monthly budget? It's much more than the check you mail to the bank or credit union every month for the next three, four, or five years. How much are you willing to pay for the privilege of driving that new car, and how much can your monthly budget handle? Minimally, you need to set aside money for:

- Monthly payment (if financing).
- Auto insurance.
- License fees.
- Normal maintenance and non-warranty repairs.
- Emission and safety repairs (used car buyers).

You need to determine how much *disposable income* you have to cover these costs. Completing the Disposable Income Budget Form in the Plan-of-Action Workbook will help generate a clear picture of your disposable income.

Today's **average** new car payment **exceeds $325 per month!** You will be making your car payments for an average of 54.6 months. One recent trend has been for dealers to advertise lower monthly payments for the first six, twelve, or eighteen months of ownership. Don't be fooled by this! A finance contract has only one monthly payment amount for its entire duration. If you are offered lower payments, all that is being done is that the dealer is paying part of each payment for a specified period. At the end of the period, you will be responsible for the entire amount of the payment each and every month. If you are not in a position to assume the full value of a payment from the beginning of a contract, you probably will not be in a much better position six, twelve, or eighteen months from now unless you know that you will be paying off additional obligations. Don't ever count on getting that raise or some other increase in your income to justify obligating yourself.

If your current car is paid for and you carry only liability insurance, your insurance rates probably will increase
when you buy a new or used car. If you are financing your
purchase, lenders will require you to carry **full** coverage
insurance (comprehensive, collision, and liability) to protect
their interest. If you pay cash for your car, you may want to
carry full coverage in order to protect your investment. If
you are paying cash and don't want to carry full coverage,
you may find your insurance is increased, because each car's
rating for insurance purposes can vary dramatically. Just
how much your insurance will increase or decrease depends
on the car you buy, where you live, and your driving record.
Sports cars and pickup trucks tend to be more expensive to
insure than sedans and wagons. Shop around for your insurance. Check with your current agent, and other companies
as well. Many people who have insured with the same company for many years believe that they are getting the best
possible rates. It is always wise to get quotes from competing
insurance companies, because one company may rate a particular car differently, resulting in a lower rate. In most
cases, insurance representatives will work with you to determine which cars offer the best insurance rates. You may find
that there are cars *very similar* to the one you are considering which offer **additional discounts and better rates because of safety features or improved repair rates** which
your choice does not offer.

Unless you are going from a newer to an older vehicle,
license fees definitely will increase, possibly by several hundred dollars a year. If your current car is more than five
years old, you are more than likely paying your state's lowest license fees, since most states base their fees on age and
value. For example, if you live in California, new-car fees
will be approximately 2% of the selling price. This means
that fees on a $15,000 car will cost about $300 for the first
year. If you have been paying only $50 a year to license your
old car, you are facing a **600% increase!** Each state differs
in how license fees are determined, so it is important to find
out what kind of increase you will be facing. Contact your

state motor vehicle licensing agency and ask how new-car license fees are determined.

If you are considering a new car, you still may have normal maintenance costs, which in most cases will not be covered by a new-car warranty but are required to keep a warranty in force (although some manufacturers do cover normal maintenance for the first one or two years of ownership). You also may encounter repairs which are not covered by the warranty. If you are a used-car purchaser, you definitely should consider possible repair costs (unless you are buying a very late model with some remaining factory warranty that is transferable).

Most states now require annual or semiannual emission tests, and many states also require safety checks to ensure that a vehicle is roadworthy. If you are a new-car buyer, this probably won't be a concern for some time. If you are a used-car buyer, this is a major concern because these costs can be extremely high. Check your state laws concerning inspections.

By considering these things, you will have a more realistic idea of the hidden costs of car ownership, and you can factor them into your monthly budget. If you really want to be thorough, you can account for increased or decreased fuel economy. The long and short of it is, there is much more to monthly payment expense than the base payment, and you're better off to consider it now than after you have purchased.

Determining Your Needs

When it comes to determining exactly what we need from a car and how much we are willing to spend to satisfy those needs, most of us end up fooling ourselves. We can become so swept up in the excitement of buying a car that all too frequently we ignore how paying for that car is going to affect our budgets.

When you consider your needs, it is very important to be practical and honest with yourself. You have seen how to determine your budget. Now let's determine which car best fits within that budget. At this point, you should have a fairly good idea of whether you will be a used-car buyer or a new-car buyer.

What you *want* from a car and *need* from a car are often completely different. Your automotive *wants* are those dreams and fantasies you experience when you look at a car. Your automotive **needs** are those things you require from a car in order to fulfill your everyday driving demands. What you need from a car is a combination of how you **use** it, how you **drive** it, and how it **fulfills your self-image.** (Face it—if all we needed was basic transportation, there would be no need for cars like Ferrari, Porsche, Maserati, or any of the other exotic nameplates!) When determining your needs, you have to consider such factors as urban vs. highway driving, carrying a few people or a troop of Cub Scouts, driving in a dry sunny climate or in a climate where the winters are cold and snowy.

Ask yourself, "Am I a hard or an easy driver?" Your current repair bills, tire wear, and gas mileage will give you a fair idea of what kind of driver you are. Finally, how do you see yourself? There are cars out there that can help satisfy your self-image and still be affordable and practical. The important thing is to realize where fantasy ends and reality begins. You must be honest and up-front with yourself about your needs, and keep those needs in clear view when determining what kind of car you will be buying. Use the checklist in your Plan-of-Action Workbook to help you determine what kind of car you should consider, based on the lifestyle you lead and the way you drive. Use it to develop a clearer picture of your **real needs.**

Another thing that will help you determine your needs is to keep a record of your driving habits with your current car. This will work best if you keep it for a period of several months, but even a few weeks will help give you an idea. You also should take a close look at your current car and make a list of things you **really like** about it and things you **really dislike** about it. You will be surprised at the picture this creates. You may even discover things you were not aware of. Perhaps you will see that you need more trunk space, or maybe you will realize that many of those power options you got last time were hardly ever used. According to statistics, **you will keep your new car six years,** so consider your needs carefully. Notice I say *needs*—not *wants*.

Who wouldn't like to have all of the goodies—but at what price? Every $1,000 in options will increase a five-year loan payment by $20 per month. Shorter-term loan payments increase even more. It's unfortunate but true—in most cases, optional equipment does not add that much value to a car at trade-in time. When your car is three, four, or five years old, a $1,000 stereo system will add *no more* to a car's trade-in value than a $350 system. Why have cruise control if you don't travel a lot? On the other hand, depending on where you live, some options are almost mandatory, and not having them will drastically affect the value of a trade. For example, if you live in a warmer climate and don't have air conditioning, your trade will be impossible to sell. Carefully examine those options that will serve your needs and not overload your payment budget.

Finally, one comment concerning dealer-installed options: *Don't ever buy them!* Any option a dealer can install, you can install or have installed and save big money. More and more dealers are loading new cars with things like paint sealant, fabric protectant, window tinting, door-edge guards, pinstriping, and more. These moneymakers are put on cars in order to increase profit margins. If a dealer were to add all of these things to a new car, the dealer's cost could be $150 to $300, but the added selling price could be $1,000 or more! This needs repeating: If the dealer can add these items, *so can you!* Dealers mark up added options 200% to 400% and even more, and most buyers are not aware of how much they are being taken. *Don't confuse "dealer installed" with "factory installed" options. If it isn't on the manufacturer's window sticker, it isn't factory installed—so don't buy it.* It's also possible that a dealer might affect a car warranty by adding things like oversize tires, lift kits, or additional suspension modifications. If you have any doubt, check the manufacturer's warranty.

Understanding the Seller's Plan

For your plan of action to be successful, you must clearly understand how sellers are motivated to achieve their goals. Basically there are two groups that sell cars:

- Car dealers.
- Private individuals.

The basic plan of action for all dealers is the same. In Step 6: Shopping for Your Next Car, be sure you carefully read "Buying from a New-Car Dealership" to fully understand the differences in the operations and where the dealer's profits come from.

The Car Dealer's Plan of Action

Dealers spend hundreds and even thousands of dollars training their sales forces. The trainers are professionals who understand the psychological profile of a car buyer, and they train the sales force to use this profile to manipulate and control the buying process.

A properly trained sales force will guide and control a potential buyer so smoothly and confidently that the buyer may not even be aware of what is happening until it's too late. Many times I sold cars to people only to have them say,

> *Gee, we only came in to look today. We didn't plan on buying now.*

The professional sales force will be able to adapt and adjust the program as required by changes in the situation. This is possible because they have been given a plan, a specific program to follow in order to maximize the profit for the dealer.

A dealer's plan of action can be condensed into six basic steps:

1. Qualify the customer.
2. Get the customer emotionally excited.
3. Gain the customer's confidence and become a friend.
4. Get the customer to raise the monthly payment and down payment budget.
5. Get mini-commitments.
6. Close the sale and deliver the car on the *first visit.*

Let's look at each of these steps and see what the dealer is attempting to do.

1. Qualify the Customer

The dealership's management team must have information in order to control you, and the sales force is trained to obtain this information by asking specific "qualifying questions" as soon as possible after making the first contact.

If you have been to a dealership, you may recognize questions such as:

WILL YOU BE TRADING YOUR CAR?

This may well be the single most important qualifying question. If a trade-in is involved, the sales manager must know as soon as possible, because all future price negotiations will be affected by this single factor. If you do have a trade, be sure to carefully read Step 5: Determining Your Trade-in's *Real* Value.

WILL YOU BE FINANCING?

Answering this question lets the sales personnel know that you have made a definite decision to buy and are ready to do so.

IS THIS CAR FOR YOU OR SOMEONE ELSE?

This may not seem like an important qualifying question, but if you respond that the car is for someone who is not present, salespeople will not spend a lot of time with you, because they assume that you will not be the person making the final decision and therefore they will not be selling a car right now.

HOW MUCH WERE YOU THINKING OF SPENDING?

With this information, the salespeople will direct you to cars that maximize their profit margin, even though you may have another model in mind.

WILL YOU BE BUYING TODAY?

When asked in a casual conversational manner, regardless of your response, this information allows the sales force to establish a time frame and will help them determine how hard to pressure you.

The variety of questions employed to get information from you is almost limitless. The key to defeating the dealer's purpose in asking any qualifying questions is to be aware that every question has some hidden intention behind it. Whenever you respond, be as vague as possible. From your initial contact all the way through the buying process, you do not want to give dealers any information which they may use to further their plan. Do not give definite yes or no responses to questions—only responses such as, *"I don't know"* or *"I'm not really sure."*

2. Get the Customer Emotionally Excited

Think back for a moment, perhaps to a time when you were a child and you saw that incredible toy, that magical plaything you **had** to have. Remember? Well, it happened to all of us at one time or another. On the other hand, think about how difficult it is to do something if you really don't want to. Almost impossible—right? Those are our emotions at work.

Dealers know that if you are not incredibly excited and involved with the new car you are considering buying, it will be very difficult to get you to pay the price they want. Manufacturers and dealers spend millions of dollars every year to advertise their cars. They want you to dream about them. They create images of beautiful people driving around in state-of-the-art machines of gleaming paint and chrome. We all see this, day in and day out, over and over again, on television and in magazines. These images are designed to stimulate our emotions and act to weaken our sensibilities. Whenever you allow your emotions to assume control, you lose. When that salesperson is speaking with you about the car you are considering, don't allow yourself to get emotionally involved. I don't care how badly you want it. Never show the salesperson that you are really excited about a particular car. When I was in sales, we always referred to people who were emotionally excited about a car as, **"Being under the ether."** These people wanted the car so badly they never realized how much they were paying for it. You might say that this wouldn't happen to you—but think again about that small child and the toy. You are only human, and you are ruled by emotion. Don't give the salesperson the chance to use your emotions against you.

3. Gain the Customer's Confidence and Become a Friend

Every truly successful salesperson has one very special ability, an ability that separates the true professional from the average. It is the ability to make customers feel so comfortable with them that they become more than a salesperson—they become a friend. This friend is someone that the customer will confide in because, if properly manipulated, customers genuinely believe that the salesperson is on their side in the buying process. It's the customers and salesperson against the dealer and the sales managers. When this rapport is properly established, salespeople can and will use this situation to their advantage. The objective is to start to establish this relationship from the first moment of contact and continue to build on it throughout the buying process. Then, when it comes time to negotiate, the salesperson will more easily persuade and manipulate the customer to achieve maximum profit in the deal. I don't want people to misconstrue my meaning here. There are many fine people in the industry whose concern and caring cannot be denied; but it is imperative that you, the consumer, remember it is still the dealer who writes that salesperson's paycheck, and the more money you pay for your car, the larger the salesperson's paycheck becomes.

4. Get the Customer to Raise the Monthly Payment and Down Payment Budget

When you go to a dealership, you have some idea of how much money you want to spend each month, and maybe even how much you have for the down payment. You believe these figures will buy you the car of your dreams. But wait! It is the salesperson's job to convince you that no matter how much you have budgeted, it is not enough.

The salesperson needs to convince you psychologically that you have underestimated the amount you need to buy the car you want. Over 60% of cars are financed; and in many cases, the payment is the most important factor. If the salesperson can convince you that your payment figure is too low and get you to increase your payment by only $20 a month for five years, that will mean an additional $1,200 to the dealer.

The same follows for down payment. If the salesperson can get you to put an additional $1,000 down, it will allow the dealer to get $20 a month closer to your budgeted payment without discounting the price of the car.

Never let anyone at a dealership talk you into increasing any of the figures you have budgeted for your new car. Once you complete this program and your plan of action, you will know **exactly** how much car your budgeted monthly payment and down payment will buy. There will be no reason for you to change your figures.

5. Get Mini-Commitments

Salespeople are trained to carefully observe potential buyers and look for **"buying signals."** These can be many things, but most often they are positive comments you make or *yes* responses to carefully worded questions a salesperson might ask. If the salesperson overhears you saying, "This is exactly what I'm looking for," or, "The color is perfect," or, "This is the most comfortable car we have driven," the salesperson knows that you are hooked and will be easier to sell. (Remember emotional excitement.) Dealers want to get you in the habit of saying *yes* as often as possible. The more frequently you respond to a question with a *yes*, the more likely you will continue to respond *yes* when asked to purchase the car. You might also watch salespeople carefully because often they will nod up and down *very slightly* as they ask questions. This is a subliminal way of getting you to say *yes* even if you are thinking *no!* At the same time you are being prepared to say *yes*, the salesperson will plant small **"seeds of doubt"** about **your** questions and comments.

> *Gee, Mr. and Mrs. Customer, that seems like an awfully small payment amount to me.*

or,

> *You know, most people put a lot more money down when they want payments that low.*

Seeds of doubt make you question the validity of your plans. They are negative responses which, if properly planted, will make it very easy for the salesperson to become the stronger negotiator. *You can weaken the dealer's negotiating position by being very noncommittal when giving a response or making any kind of comment about a car. It is best if you never say yes to anything! Be as vague as possible.*

6. Close the Sale and Deliver the Car on the *First Visit*

In today's car market, it is very important for the dealer to sell you on the first visit because the odds are that you will not be back a second time. There are more new-car choices today than ever before, and more dealerships from which you can choose. U.S. auto manufacturers are producing cars at less than 80% capacity. Dealers are hungry and competition is fierce, especially with the advent of what I call "used-new-car dealers." These are the major car rental companies, such as Budget and National, who no longer send their used rental fleet to auction, but sell directly to the public through their own sales outlets. (In Step 6, Shopping for Your Next Car, carefully read "Buying from a Rental-Car Resale Lot.")

Once dealers get you to agree to purchase a car, **they always want you to take immediate delivery**. This is because there is always the chance that you might change your mind or happen to stop by one last dealership and maybe get a better deal. You can't imagine how many deals have been lost because another dealer beat the price by $50—or even $25! Salespeople will apply pressure to convince you that theirs is the right deal and you need to take delivery **now**. Right for the dealer, maybe—but not necessarily you.

Even if the car you have selected isn't ready, the salesperson may say something like,

> *Let's get the paperwork out of the way so when you come back you won't have to wait.*

Once you have signed a contract and driven a new car off the lot, **you are an owner.** It is yours—and make no mistake about that! A car isn't something you can return just because you decide you don't like it. (Some states do have "lemon laws" to protect customers from poorly manufactured products, but don't count on this.) Once a decision has been made to buy, the dealer wants things wrapped up as quickly as possible. This will keep you from having second thoughts. **You decide when to take delivery of your new car. The dealer can't make you take delivery until you are ready. It is fine to go ahead and take delivery if you are ready and satisfied, but you make the choice! Saying you want a night to think it over will make the dealer uneasy about the security of the deal. Let the dealer sweat a little. That is just where you want him.**

The Private Seller's Plan of Action

The plan of action of private sellers is not nearly as extensive—but still, they have one. Individuals sell cars for one of three reasons:

1. They no longer need the car.
2. It needs work and they don't want or can't afford to have it done.
3. They are forced to sell for financial reasons.

Before you consider buying from a private party, carefully read Step 8, Selecting and Test-Driving a Car (especially the section on checking out a used car); and in Step 10, the section on how to write a bill of sale.

Let's take a closer look at each reason.

1. They no longer need the car.

Perhaps they have acquired another car and the one they are selling is just taking up space. They may have elected not to trade it in because they felt they could get a better price for it. It may be that illness or age has forced them to stop driving. This is an acceptable situation, provided it is in fact the *only* reason for selling the car. If you consider this type of used car, be sure the seller has no hidden agenda.

2. It needs work and they don't want or can't afford to have it done.

This is a major reason for many people, and one they will rarely—if ever—volunteer to tell you. As a car ages, repair costs increase in direct proportion to the care it has been given over the years. Often, the neglect gets to a point where the owner just doesn't want to deal with it. Sellers may give slight indications that "It needs little things here and there," but that's about all they are willing to say. Be wary of ads that read, "Needs work" unless you are looking for something to restore or rebuild. You don't want to depend on one of these cars.

3. They are forced to sell for financial reasons.

Unfortunately, with the economy the way it is, many people have found themselves in financial difficulties, and sometimes the only way out is to sell the car and get something less expensive. If too much is owing on it, a dealer probably won't give them enough to purchase another car, so they have only one alternative. The only caution here is that sometimes when people know they are going to be forced to sell their cars, they neglect or even abuse them because they simply don't care about them any more.

Knowing Your Financial Position

The amount of car your budgeted monthly payment can buy depends entirely on the loan interest rate you qualify for. Simply put:

> *The lower your interest rate, the more you can finance for your budgeted monthly payment.*

The interest rate you pay will be determined by several factors, but the three most important are:

- **Your credit record**
- **The amount of your down payment**
- **Where you borrow your money**

Only you and your creditors really know the condition of your credit report. In general, if you have always paid your bills promptly, have no legal judgments or tax liens, and don't have a lot of outstanding debt (referred to as "income-to-debt ratio"), then you should qualify for the lowest possible consumer auto-loan rate a lender offers because you are considered a very good risk. If you have no established credit record, are young, or have some late payments or other blemishes on your credit report, in all probability you will not qualify for the best rates. (If you are young and have never financed a car, some manufacturers will offer special "first-time buyer" programs to assist you.) If your length of employment is less than two years, the rates may not be as favorable (unless you changed jobs but remained in the same field).

If you are going to be buying from a dealer, it is important for you to know exactly what interest rate you do qualify for before you visit any dealership. When I was in sales, I was often told by managers,

> *Most people don't know how good their credit is, and if you tell them that 15% or more is the best interest rate they can get, they probably will not question it.*

This is sad but true; and when it comes time to sign on the dotted line, most people are so excited that they will accept almost anything they are told. Don't believe it! What you must do is go to *at least two* banks or credit unions and apply for a "preapproved" auto loan. Once your application has been approved, a loan officer will let you know the interest rate you have qualified for and, in some cases, the maximum amount you may borrow. Once you know this, there is no reason for a dealership finance department to rip you off on interest rates—and if they can, they will.

Due to changes in the tax laws concerning deduction of interest you pay, it is important to discuss an alternative to consumer auto loans. Since interest paid on an auto loan is *no longer tax deductible*, if you are a home owner with available equity in your home, it may be to your advantage to consider the possibility of a "home-equity credit line." In most cases, the interest on this type of loan is *fully tax deductible.* Home-equity loans are usually at rates lower than auto loans, and the money is at your disposal when you want it. Of course, manufacturers often offer special low-interest rates; but when you consider the savings you will experience by having that tax deduction, there is little advantage to lower interest rates which are not tax deductible. If you use a home-equity credit line, you will simply pay cash to the dealer.

If you do wind up with a conventional auto loan, you probably will need some kind of down payment, especially if you are purchasing a used car. Banks and credit unions usually give you a better rate with a larger down payment, and this also will reduce monthly payments. Many lenders require a minimum of 20% down, unless you have exceptional credit. When applying for any auto loan, be sure to ask about down payment requirements. Down payment can be a combination of three things:

- **Cash**
- **Factory rebates**
- **Your trade-in**

Some credit unions do not consider a manufacturer's rebate as part of your down payment and may require additional money from you.

Where you borrow your money can be as important as your credit rating and down payment. There are three major sources for financing today:

- **Banks**
- **Credit unions**
- **Dealership financing**

Bank Financing

This is always a good choice for a loan. In fact, almost 44% of **new** car loans are through banks. You own bank may be an excellent source for a loan, especially if your relationship with that bank has been established for some time. Your bank knows how you handle your finances, pay your bills, and how much money you maintain in your accounts. Often, you will get a reduction in the interest rate if you allow the bank to automatically deduct your payment from your account each month. If you have a substantial savings account with your bank, you might choose to borrow against your savings and get a reduced loan rate. But be careful of this. Be sure to ask if this will tie up funds, making them unavailable for the duration of the loan. If you choose to consider the home-equity credit line, your personal bank or mortgage company will be an excellent place to begin.

Financing Through a Credit Union

Statistics indicate that approximately 21% of *new* car loans are financed through credit unions. If you belong to or can join a credit union, probably you will get the lowest rates there—but not always. If your credit union operates through your employer, you will have the added advantage of payroll deduction. Credit unions sometimes finance people with less than desirable credit histories if they have been affiliated with the same employer and credit union for a number of years. Often, credit unions will sponsor sales through specified dealers to ensure their members of guaranteed pricing on cars.

Dealership Financing

Dealer or manufacturer financing now accounts for 32% of all new-car loans. This has become a major profit maker for the dealers. The only time you should *ever* consider letting a dealer arrange your financing is when a manufacturer is offering special low financing rates, such as 2.9%, 4.9%, or 9.9%. However, beware when these rates are offered, because many dealers will use these low rates as leverage to keep the price of the car higher. You may hear something like,

> With rates like these, we can't afford to discount the car.

What can I say? They are lying, pure and simple. One of the best months that I experienced in car sales was September 1986, when General Motors was offering financing as low as 2.9% on new cars for 24 months. *24 months!* People were so hungry to get low financing rates that they didn't seem to care how much they paid for the car. That September, I made over $8,000! That's right! *Over $8,000 for one month's work!* Another salesperson made more than $14,000 during the same period—all because buyers wanted to get low finance rates. *Do not fall for this trap.* You must understand that anything the dealer does or arranges for you will cost you money. This includes arranging financing. If dealers arrange your financing through local lenders, they are simply acting as the middleman. The dealer may even arrange your loan with your own bank! The dealer borrows the money for you at one rate, and lends it back to you at a higher rate. The difference is called "finance reserve." For example, the dealer may borrow the money at 10% (called the dealer's "buy rate"), and then arrange your loan at 13%. The 3% difference is simply more profit for the dealer. In today's market, many dealers are making more money on the finance reserve profit than on the car profit—which is why dealers are so eager to give you "convenient one-stop financing." Not only do they make a profit on the new car, they make profit on your financing! What could be better for the dealer? Plenty, if the dealer's finance manager is any good, because they also will talk you into other things, such as extended warranties on the care, and life/disability insurance on the loan. These items are extremely costly to consumers. If you want to get insurance to protect your loan, check with your own insurance agent. Dealers make tremendous commissions from insurance companies when they sell you contract insurance.

Another point to remember is that *special dealer financing rates are usually only on the models that are not selling well. There is never a need to place special rates on the hot sellers, and you can be sure the dealer won't.*

How Much Can You Finance?

Once you have your preapproved loan and know the rates you qualify for, you will be able to determine how much you can finance for the payment you have budgeted. In order to do this, turn to the interest rate charts in the back of this book. Find the rate closest to your qualifying rate. (If your exact rate isn't shown, choose a rate slightly higher rather than one that is slightly lower.) The column on the left shows the total "Amount you can finance." The remaining four columns are for terms of 24, 36, 48, and 60 months. Each of these columns lists a monthly payment that is close to your budgeted payment. To find it, simply run your finger down each column until you see the payment closest to yours. Once you find the payment, move your finger to the left, and you will see the "amount you can finance" for the payment you have budgeted for that specific term. You will find that the longer the term, the larger the amount financed. This means, the more car you can buy and still maintain your payment. Look at the illustration below, and you will see how simple it is.

The total amount you can finance for the term selected, added to the total amount of down payment, consumer rebates, and/or trade-in you have, will equal the *total "Out-the-Door Amount"* you can spend for your new car *without affecting your payment budget.* (Refer to the "Out-the-Door" Price Worksheet in your Plan-of-Action Workbook.) "Out-the-door" means total including all taxes, license fees, and any extras the dealer finance manager might talk you into. If this figure is exceeded, your budgeted monthly payment will go up.

Interest Rate: 11.9%

Amount you can can finance:	Monthly payment amount for:			
	24 months	36 months	48 months	60 months
$ 6,000.00	$ 283.00	$ 200.00	$ 158.00	$ 134.00
6,500.00	**306.00**	216.00	171.00	145.00
7,000.00	330.00	233.00	184.00	156.00
7,500.00	353.00	249.00	198.00	167.00
8,000.00	377.00	266.00	211.00	178.00
8,500.00	400.00	282.00	224.00	189.00
9,000.00	424.00	**299.00**	237.00	200.00
9,500.00	447.00	316.00	250.00	211.00
10,000.00	471.00	332.00	263.00	222.00
10,500.00	494.00	349.00	276.00	234.00
11,000.00	518.00	365.00	290.00	245.00
11,500.00	541.00	382.00	**303.00**	256.00
12,000.00	565.00	399.00	316.00	267.00
12,500.00	588.00	415.00	329.00	278.00
13,000.00	612.00	432.00	342.00	289.00
13,500.00	635.00	448.00	355.00	**300.00**

(If your **loan rate is 11.9%** and your **budgeted payment** is $300.00, you can finance **$6,500 for 24 months, $9,000 for 36 months, $11,500 for 48 months, and $13,500 for 60 months.**)

Determining Your Trade-in's *Real* Value

If you don't have much cash available for down payment and there are no factory rebates available from the manufacturer (and if you're buying a used car, there won't be), you may be tempted to trade in the car you are driving now. There may appear to be good reasons for doing this.

- It's a hassle to sell your car yourself.
- You don't want strangers coming to your home.
- Someone might have an accident while test-driving your car.
- What happens if the potential buyer needs to finance?
- You still owe money on your car.

But there is *one* very good reason for *not* trading:

You are throwing money away!!

If you intend to trade in your car, I promise that in most cases, you will get **less than half** of what you think your car is worth. You will be much better off selling your trade yourself or having a friend sell it for you. However, if you insist on trading it in, there are things you **must** do in order to maintain control and still get the best deal on a car. The most important one is this:

Never tell a salesperson you have a trade until you have agreed upon a price for the new car.

The moment you tell a salesperson that you have a car to trade in, you have lost control. You have totally changed the direction negotiations will take. The sales staff will alter every step they take once negotiations begin. You **must** train yourself to say *no* regardless of how often you are asked about a trade-in. Remember that qualifying question:

Will you be trading in a car today?

This innocent-sounding question will cost you more than you can imagine. Remember the dealer's plan. The dealer wants information from you—information that will be used to manipulate you. Of course, while the sales personnel are trying to find out whether you have a trade, they may tell you that they **need** good trades like yours and that they will give you **top dollar** for it; but once you tell them you have a trade and how much you think it is worth, the story will change. Once negotiations start, the new attitude will be very different, with "seeds of doubt" like,

> *That seems like a lot for such an old model!*
>
> *You know, we had one like yours a while back, and we couldn't give it away! There just isn't a market for it.*

Dealers do this because **no matter what is said, a trade-in is worth only wholesale, and that is all you are going to get for it.** You have in mind your trade's retail value, and the dealer looks at it from only a wholesale point of view.

If a car is to be traded, the dealership desk manager needs to know as soon as possible. It is even better if the manager can find out how much you think you want for it, because he may have to keep the price up on the new car in order to allow for your trade-in. At the very least, you will get only a token discount. The dealer must do this because if you want more than actual wholesale trade-in value, that difference (between what you want and what your car is worth at wholesale) must come out of the profit of the new car. Any time a dealer gives you what you want for your trade and what you want exceeds its actual wholesale value, they are "over-allowing." Over-allowing is simply showing you more for your trade than it is worth in order to satisfy you. The bottom line is, you are going to get only the wholesale value and no more! No matter how they dress up the figures, the end result is the same.

Be realistic! Know the actual wholesale value of your trade.

You are fooling no one but yourself if you believe the dealer is giving you what you want for your trade. I don't care what kind of car you drive, what kind of shape it is in, or how popular it may be. The dealer is going to take it in trade at wholesale, and then sell it for a profit. Think about this: If the dealer gives you retail and then sells it at retail, where is the profit? The dealer will always have to do some reconditioning, and in the process there will be expenses. Those expenses will have to be added to the cost of your trade—and how can dealers do that if they are giving you retail?

OK, then. How do you arrive at a *fair wholesale value* for your car? It will take a little work, but there are two things you *don't* do:

- **Don't look in the paper** to see what cars like yours are being advertised for. Remember, these are retail "asking" prices and have nothing in common with wholesale prices.

- **Don't ask your friends who think they are experts on cars.** They probably know less than you do about your car's value.

The first step in determining your car's fair wholesale value is to go to a bank or library and ask to see a copy of the **current** "blue book." These books are published every two to three months, and there are issues for different regions of the country. Lenders will use them to help establish a car's **wholesale loan value.** This is the amount a lender will lend a potential buyer on a given car. Bear in mind that the **loan value IS NOT the trade-in value,** but it is a starting point because dealers will use the same "blue book" when they appraise your trade-in.

Several other factors **will** affect your trade-in's value:

- At the bottom of every page of the "blue book" are the words **"Deduct for Reconditioning."** Believe me, the dealer will. Mileage will affect a great deal if it is high, but the dealer won't allow extra if it is low.

- Market conditions also will mean less money. If there are hundreds of cars like yours currently being traded in, the value will drop because of an excess in the marketplace.

As a general rule, most trade-ins will be appraised from **$1,000 to $3,000 *below*** the wholesale value.

Often, a dealer will try to "lowball" your trade-in's appraisal. Lowballing is a term used when a customer is offered far less than the trade is actually worth. The dealer does this for two reasons:

- If you have asked for a retail trade value, the lowball figure will be used to throw you off balance and make you question how valid your figures are. The dealer hopes this will get you to lower the amount you want for your trade.

- If the dealer can get you to fall for a lowball appraisal, you will be giving up your trade for much less than it is worth, and the difference will become part of the profit of the sale. All too often, customers fall for this and lose money.

The most accurate way to determine your car's trade-in value will require some work on your part. First, you will want to clean and polish your car (detail it). If you can afford to spend $50 to $100, take it to a professional detail shop. You want the car looking its very best. Next, drive it to *at least three* used-car lots. Many times these lots will advertise, "We Buy Cars." Tell the owner or manager that you want to sell your car, and ask how much they will give you. The person will appraise your car just as a dealer taking it in trade will do, and will name a dollar amount that they will pay for it. Get the name of the person making the bid, and ask how long they will honor the bid. Even better—if you can, get the bid in writing (although most used-car dealers probably will hesitate to do this). Repeat this procedure at the other two dealers you have selected. If you have gone to established dealers and your car isn't a piece of junk, when you are finished you should have three bids that are fairly close (unless one was trying to lowball you, hoping to' get your car cheaply). Dealers always need clean used cars. They will want your car, and it will be in their best interest to appraise it fairly. If the three appraisals are close, then you have an idea of your trade's *"fair wholesale market value."*

When you are negotiating the price of the new car you wish to buy and you have agreed upon a selling price for the new car, *then and only then* should you tell a salesperson that you do in fact have a trade. This probably will upset the salesperson and the desk manager. Assure them that you have every intention of buying the new car; you simply want their used-car manager to appraise your trade. If the dealer's appraisal is within $100 of the independent appraisals, let the dealer have your car in trade. If there is a big difference, then calmly tell the dealer that you have gotten three other appraisals which are much higher. Assure the dealer that just as soon as you sell your trade to one of the other dealers, you will return to buy the new car. The dealership personnel will not want you to leave without "tying up" the new car with a deposit—but don't do that. Tell the dealer, "If you can get closer to the three figures I already have, I will trade in my car and take delivery of the new car right now." This will get the dealer to look more closely at your trade and not play any more games. Believe me, they want to sell and deliver to you *now*. At this point, it's all right to tell the dealer what the other appraisals are, because it will let him know where he has to be in order to finalize the deal. As long as the appraisals you have received are good, the dealer should go for it. You might even add $100 to the other appraisals; who knows—you may get it. (That would mean you "highballed" the dealer!)

If you must trade in your car, be smart, do your homework, and it will mean money in your pocket— not the dealer's.

Warning: Be sure to take an extra ignition key with you to give to the appraiser. Never give them your regular keys, because sometimes the dealer will try to hold onto them to keep you from leaving.

Shopping for Your Next Car

If you are a new-car buyer, your sources for finding a car are more limited than if you are a used-car buyer.

Let's look first at new-car buying sources.

You have three basic sources for acquiring a new car:

- **New-car dealership.**
- **Auto broker or buying service.**
- **Leasing company.**

Notice I referred to *acquiring* and not *buying* because when you lease a car, you are not actually buying. Leasing is covered more fully in another chapter and is mentioned here only to show it as one source for new cars.

By definition, a "new" car is one that has never previously been sold or registered to an individual or company and the title is still the "Manufacturer's Statement of Origin." This statement of origin, or "MSO," is the document the manufacturer provides to selling dealers for each new vehicle that is shipped to them. These are negotiable documents often resembling regular ownership titles, and they must be executed and legally documented under very strict guidelines. If you, an individual, buy a new car from a dealer, when the vehicle is registered to you and/or a lender, the MSO is delivered to your state licensing agency, which in turn will issue a new title in your name. This will occur only if you buy from a new-car dealer. If you buy from a broker, in effect you are buying a used car because the broker first must buy the car from a dealer and then transfer ownership to you. So, which direction should you go? If, by the definition outlined above, you absolutely must have a "new" car, then you must buy from a dealer. However, if being the second registered owner on a title history doesn't matter, then you may do well to consider a broker.

Let's take a closer look at dealers and brokers and exactly what they do for you.

Buying from a New-Car Dealership

A *new-car franchised dealership* is where the majority of people go to buy new cars. These are complete one-stop facilities offering both sales and service. In today's economy, it is becoming more and more difficult for a dealership to survive if it has only one make to sell, so many dealers are franchised to sell more than one make of car. The dealer maintains an extensive new-car inventory and also acts as a factory representative if you choose to special-order your car directly from the manufacturer. New-car dealers have three primary areas where they make money:

- Car sales.
- Service repairs.
- Body shop repairs.

In most dealerships, there are two separate departments handling new car sales: the "retail sales department" (which is

the department most people are familiar with) and the "fleet
sales department" (which many people have heard of but
may not fully understand). The retail sales department deals
with single-unit purchases; in other words, one person going
in and buying one car. The fleet sales department usually
deals with individuals buying several cars at one time, usually for company use. In most cases, the average buyer will
not be aware that there is a fleet sales department on the
premises.

Most new-car dealers hire their retail salespeople and
pay them on a commission basis, while the fleet salespeople
may work on a smaller commission basis or be paid a flat-
rate amount for each car they sell because they deal in volume. Commission pay structures are established by each
dealership and usually are a percentage of either the *gross
profit* or the *net profit* in the sale. Most dealership commission plans are calculated on a sliding scale, meaning that the
more cars a person sells, the higher the rate of commission
that is paid. For example, let's say that the dealer agrees to
pay a salesperson 20% of the gross profit on the first ten
cars sold every month, and then 25% on the next five cars,
and 30% on all sales after that. Some dealers also offer
bonuses and incentives to the sales staff to entice them to
sell older stock from inventory. Fleet sales department payment plans are different because they sell volume more than
profit. Many manufacturers base a dealership's future al-
location (the number of cars a dealer will be allowed to
order) on total number of units sold. It is important to the
dealer to sell as many cars as possible during the reporting
period, and the fleet sales department will help ensure this.

Most brokers and buying services, as well as leasing
companies, work only through the fleet sales department
even if they are buying only one car—so why can't you?
Most fleet departments don't work with the general public
because individuals buy only once every five or six years,
while a broker or leasing company may buy 60 or more cars
per year. Again, it's volume that matters to fleet sales departments. This doesn't mean that you can't work through
a fleet department to buy, but you may have a hard time

getting some dealers to allow it. If they don't, go somewhere else until you find a dealer who will.

In the past year, dealers have used some dramatic tactics to clean up their reputation and boost sales. One dealership in Florida fired all sales personnel and had customers work directly with a group of managers, because statistics tell us that consumers hate to deal with salespeople. The only problem I have with this is that those managers got to be managers because they were among the top performers in the sales department and probably made consistently higher gross profits than the other salespeople. Managers are the cream of the crop, and they know how to manipulate customers and close deals better than anyone. Another problem is that initially, many people may believe they *are* getting a better deal because they are not dealing with a salesperson. This may be true; but as consumers get lulled into a false sense of security by the new selling concept, they may tend to drop their guard. Gradually, the dealers may wind up making more money by virtue of the more experienced manager/negotiator and the buyer's feeling that since there is no salesperson, the deal will be better. The salesperson is still there; the name has just been changed to "manager."

Another new tactic which may instill a false sense of security among consumers is the "best-price sticker dealership." These are dealerships that say they are putting the ***"bottom-dollar lowest price"*** right on the window of a car to eliminate the hassle of negotiating. Get real, people! There may be some dealers out there who will put bottom-dollar figures on cars for a short time; but once consumers start to believe this is in fact the bottom line, the dealers will start adding $100 here or $200 there, and soon it's the same old game again. The philosophy of most dealership management is, "There are people out there who still will expect a discount, so we need to leave ourselves room to give a little extra when needed."

A third new tactic being used is the "no-commission-sales department." Salespeople are paid a salary instead of commission; however, the salary schedule probably is still based on performance, and very possibly the gross profit.

The dealer may not actually pay a commission, but he can create a very good bonus program. For example, let's say the salesperson's salary is $2,000 per month provided that person sells ten cars. If the person sells 15, perhaps the dealer pays a bonus; but more important, if the gross profit average reaches a certain level, the salesperson may qualify for an even bigger bonus.

You have to remember that really good salespeople will always want to work on some type of commission or bonus program because they have the potential to make tremendous money. If a dealer cuts off the money potential, the good sales professionals will go where they can make that tremendous money; and in the process, the dealership will lose its best producers—so, somehow the dealer must entice the best salespeople not to leave. The dealers also hope that they will make up the difference by selling other products and services. Nothing that the dealers do is going to change their image—which is why some people deal with brokers.

Buying from a Broker

A broker is nothing more than a "middleman," an intermediary between a potential buyer and a dealership. There are three important things to remember when considering a broker:

1. Brokers are **not** authorized by the manufacturers to sell their products. They are not franchised new-car dealers.

2. Brokers do **not** maintain a sizable inventory for you to choose from. However, often they do have display cars from several different dealers for comparison purposes.

3. Brokers do not perform any maintenance or warranty repair services.

The primary service a broker offers is convenience and the appearance of a "no hassle" environment. Many people who do not want to work with traditional dealership sales personnel may choose to work through a broker. People perceive they will get the best possible deal on a new car by working through a broker. Maybe so—but maybe not! One important thing to remember is that most employees at brokerage houses used to be car sales personnel themselves, and they know the tricks of the trade only too well.

Another consideration is that most brokers also pay their sales personnel on a commission basis, just like a dealer. They also offer very high bonuses for add-on sales such as window tint, paint sealant, upholstery protector, and undercoating. Remember, these are high-profit items that will cost you dearly and put money in the salesperson's pocket.

The broker's sales representative will meet with you, the prospective buyer, to discuss what you want to purchase. There may be brochures to assist in the selection process; but in most cases, they won't have a car for you to look at. Once a decision has been made, the sales representative may suggest that you go to a local dealership for a test drive, but not to attempt to negotiate or buy. Once you have decided what car you want, the broker will work with a dealership fleet sales department for the best deal he can get. The broker then adds a profit to the purchase price, and the resulting figure will be the price the consumer will pay. If the price is agreeable, the buyer will give the broker a deposit, and the broker will arrange to get the car for the buyer. Often, brokers also assist in arranging financing. Many of the larger brokerage companies will work with local lenders to arrange special sales which are supposed to guarantee the lowest possible prices.

There is one caution to consider at this point: Brokers are not in business for the fun of it. They are out to make profits, just as in any other business. Many people, assuming they will get the best deal, often relax too much, let down their defenses, and wind up paying more for a car from a broker than they would from a dealer.

If you are in the market for a *used car,* you have a much wider field of possibilities:

- New-car dealer's "used-car department"
- Independent used-car lot

- Rental-car company resale lot
- Private parties selling their own cars
- Bank selling repossessed cars
- Public auto auctions
- IRS and government sales
- Company fleet sales

Buying from a New-Car Dealer's "Used-Car Department"

Many people who do choose to trade in their cars often trade like makes and models; Buick owners will trade for Buick products, and Ford owners will trade for Ford products. This provides a dealership with a better quality inventory of used cars than the independent used-car lot (although not always). Large new-car dealerships have better service facilities. If they have warranted the used car you purchase, this could be an important consideration. As a rule, new-car dealerships keep only the very best of the trade-in cars they receive. The rest will be wholesaled to independent car lots or taken to an auto auction. Most new-car dealers do not want to damage their public image by selling poorer-quality used cars.

Buying from an Independent Used-Car Lot

Independent used-car dealers are not high on my shopping list unless they are well established, have been in the same location for more than ten years, and have a proven track record of customer satisfaction and few (if any) Better Business Bureau complaints or cases filed against them in Small Claims Court. It is the independent used-car dealers that get the "less than desirable" new-car dealer trade-ins. These dealers often have no service facilities and probably offer no warranties on their products. Because the only way they make their profits is by selling cars, their prices are higher, and they are less flexible when negotiating and probably use stronger high-pressure sales tactics and make verbal commitments that never materialize and will disappear after delivery. Many independent dealers offer to finance cars for people who have poor credit. The interest rates they charge are extremely high; in fact, in most cases they probably will reach the legal limit set by their state. Consumers with poor credit histories often feel they have no choice but to pay. Independent lot owners usually demand a down payment equal to their investment in the car so that if something happens, they will not have lost any money on the deal. Avoid these dealers!

Buying from a Rental-Car Resale Lot

In recent years, major rental-car companies have opened their own sales facilities. Hertz, Avis, National, Budget, and other rental companies buy their fleets of cars directly from the manufacturers at substantial savings. They may pay even **less** than dealers do for comparably equipped models. The reason for giving rental companies such prices is simple. Automakers know that every individual who rents a car is a potential buyer, and the more cars automakers can get placed into a rental company's fleet, the more consumers will drive them and, subsequently, the more cars the automaker will sell. For this reason, automakers vie for the attention of rental companies by offering greater incentives to entice these companies to purchase their cars.

Most rental companies keep their cars in use until they have an average of 12,000 to 15,000 miles on them. Until recently, once the rental cars had accumulated this mileage, they were taken to an auto auction to be sold to dealers. The dealers who bought these cars then placed them on their used-car lots and resold them. At some point, rental company executives must have decided that they were missing out on a potential gold mine—and they were. They decided to resell their cars themselves, and started opening sales lots in major cities throughout the country. These facilities advertise current and late-model cars at substantial savings over identical cars sold by a dealer. This is possible because of the low price the company paid for the car to start with, and the fact that by renting the car out, the rental company has regained the major portion of the purchase price.

Many times, cars are advertised for thousands of dollars less than comparably equipped new cars. Dealers attempt to discredit these cars by telling potential buyers that people who drive rental cars tend to abuse them because they don't care what condition the car is in after they return it to the rental company. This isn't true. Rental companies take **better** care of their fleets because the cars see continuous use. The service intervals are closer together, and their cars are thoroughly inspected and very carefully maintained. Rental companies must take exceptional care of the cars they rent because of their liability if serious injury or death occurs as a result of improper or careless maintenance.

There are a couple of potential drawbacks to purchasing a rental-fleet car. Foremost is the fact that any car you purchase will be a used car. If you must have a new car, rental fleet cars are out. However, if you want to avoid the serious depreciation that always occurs when purchasing a new car, rental-fleet cars offer a great alternative. Another problem will be selection. Not every make and model is available— but most consumers will be able to find cars that will satisfy their needs. The only real possible problems are **service** and **warranty**. Most rental companies **do not** have service facilities to take care of problems (although they may be affiliated with companies that handle service needs). Most rental companies provide free or additional-cost extended warranties to protect your car; and in many cases, the manufacturer's warranty will be in effect and can be transferred. There are questions that definitely need to be asked.

If you are going to consider the rental-fleet car, you must be prepared to negotiate differently. There will be no way for you to determine how much the rental company has paid for the car or how much their actual cost may be. Rental companies make some tremendous profits from people who assume they are getting the "rock-bottom price." **Never** assume this. Always negotiate very hard for the best possible price. If you see one of these companies advertising "Double your down payment" or "Double your trade-in value" or "Take $4,000 off the price of any car in stock," you can bet that they have drastically marked up the prices of their cars in order to accommodate these outrageous claims! Also remember this: There will **never, never** be **any** kind of manufacturer rebates or incentives on these cars no matter what **anyone** may tell you, because they are nothing more than **used cars.** Don't fall for these tactics. Shop around and negotiate very carefully, and you may be a very satisfied customer.

How do you decide if you should buy a rental-fleet car? If you want a clean, well-maintained, current or late-model car at savings of up to 50%, I strongly recommend considering one. But if you want a brand-new car, pass these by.

Buying from Private Parties Selling Their Own Cars

In my opinion, this is the best source for a used-car purchase—given the proper approach. There are thousands of terrific used cars offered for sale by private parties. There also are as many pieces of junk, so you must be very careful and thorough when you shop.

You may find some hurdles in your path when buying from a private party. For example, if you plan to finance, it may make some private sellers nervous because they want to sell their cars as soon as possible and may be afraid it will take some time for you to arrange for financing. If you have prepared yourself and obtained preapproved financing, this should alleviate some of the seller's concerns.

When you are considering buying from a private party, be careful. Many people who place ads may make claims about their cars which are not entirely true. These may be innocent errors because private party sellers are not professionals. For example, an advertisement may read, "new brakes." This may mean that the owner had the brake pads or shoes replaced—but you may interpret it to mean not only new pads and shoes but also wheel cylinders, brake calipers, master cylinder, power-brake booster, and even new brake drums or brake rotors. If an advertisement reads "recent tune-up," does it mean a **major** tune-up, which can cost several hundred dollars, or a **minor** tune-up, which may cost only $30 to $100? Maybe it just means that the owner put new spark plugs in the car. Everyone's definition of "new," "recent," or "complete" is different, so if you are in doubt about what a seller means, get exact clarification—and if you are still unsure, ask to see receipts to substantiate the claims. Private-party sellers are liable for the claims they make in an advertisement, just as dealers are.

Private-party sellers do have one advantage that dealers do not. In most cases, they have only one or two cars to sell and, depending on the type of car, they may have more prospective buyers wanting to negotiate. This will be especially true if the car is a model that is in high demand by the public.

When considering a private-party seller, look for a "one-owner" seller who purchased the car new. Also try to find an owner who has kept extensive records of service and repairs. This will give you an opportunity to determine whether there have been any ongoing service problems which may cost you money in the future. People who tell you that they have complete service records generally are people who have maintained their cars very well and want to be sure that the person who buys the car will continue to take the same care. These are people who think of their cars as more than transportation.

Some private-party sellers think their cars are worth far more than they actually are and will advertise them for ridiculous prices. A little research into comparable models that are also offered for sale should quickly tell you whether they are out of line and you should look elsewhere.

Buying a Repossessed Car

Most banks and finance companies have cars that they have had to repossess because the buyers failed to make the payments. The lenders usually sell these cars at dealer auctions, but from time to time they advertise them for sale to the general public. You may find a bargain here, because often the lender is trying to collect only the remaining balance due minus interest charges. It depends on how long the buyer originally financed the car and how many payments were made. If the buyer financed for five years and kept the car for only 12 to 18 months, then the payoff will probably be too great to make the deal attractive. However, if the finance term was four years or less and the buyer had kept it for 18 to 30 months, then there may be a very good opportunity waiting for you. Some people don't like to buy a repossessed car because it appears that they are taking advantage of another's misfortunes. This may well be true—but I promise you, if such an opportunity arises and you don't take advantage of it, someone will.

Many times lenders will sell a repossessed car on a "sealed-bid" basis. This means that you would look at the car, determine how much you would be willing to pay for it, and then give the lender your bid in a sealed envelope which would be opened with other sealed bids at a predetermined date and time. At that time, whoever made the highest bid would buy the car.

One word of caution concerning repossessed cars. Sometimes when people know that their cars will be repossessed, they abuse and tear them up because they simply don't care about them. A repossession damages a person's credit history badly, and most people realize this fact. Damaging the car is often the owner's revenge against the lender. Bear in mind that the damage may not be visible. The owner may attempt to sabotage the engine or some other vital component, which may not break down immediately but will in a month or two, after the car has been resold. If there is no warranty on the repossessed car, the new owner will have no recourse and will have to bear the expense of the repair. If you do consider a bank repossession, be sure to have the car thoroughly checked by a qualified repair facility. If the lender won't allow this, walk away and save yourself some headaches.

Buying at a Public Auto Auction

There are two types of auto auctions, "dealer-only" and "public." In dealer-only auctions, only licensed auto dealers are able to obtain entry and buy cars. A public auto auction is open to all interested parties. Many people believe that they will get super deals at the public auto auctions, but this is not always the case. Generally, the cars found at public auto auctions are those that are difficult to sell through any other means. This does not necessarily mean that the cars are not good, but perhaps they are high-mileage cars or cars that must be sold quickly. One of the problems with auctions is that in most cases you don't have the opportunity to have the car thoroughly examined, and often there isn't even an opportunity to test-drive a car. If there is a test-drive track, it may be too short to allow for proper evaluation of a car's running condition.

If you are seriously planning to go to an auto auction, take along a qualified technician to help you. It may cost you some money, but it may well save you thousands of dollars.

Buying at IRS and Government Sales

These sales are widely advertised on radio and television and in newspapers. They are not for people who need to find a car immediately because they do not take place often.

Many people advertise that they will show you the way to buy a Mercedes, Jaguar, Ferrari, Corvette, and other exotic car for $100.00. These people make their money selling lists of agencies that auction cars that were seized by the Internal Revenue Service, drug enforcement agencies, and other governmental groups. You don't need to pay someone for this information. Simply go to the public library and ask for information on how to get on the mailing lists for these various agencies. Your local sheriff and police departments also hold such auctions, although not on the same scale. These auctions may take place only every six months. At best, you are gambling your money because in most cases you will not have an opportunity to drive the cars and properly evaluate them. For people who have time and energy to invest, this can be an interesting game to play, with potential rewards for their efforts, but it is not for the average car buyer.

Buying from Company Fleet Sales

These cars are not unlike rental-fleet purchases. Many government agencies and major corporations buy thousands of cars for business use. Periodically, they sell off older cars to make way for newer cars. The agencies advertise in local newspapers' "legal notices" sections and regular used-car ads, listing a date and time of sale. All of the cars will be available to be looked at, and the sales will be either by sealed bid or open auction to the highest bidder. In most cases there will be many cars all basically alike, the same color and with the equipment. Usually they will all be fairly high-mileage cars because they have been used for daily business. These cars can offer a good value provided they have been properly cared for by the company or agency. The biggest danger is that you have no way of knowing how the cars have been treated by the various drivers. Caution is the word here. If you can clearly determine the condition of the car, proceed. If you can't, avoid it.

Conclusion

In the final analysis, if you want a new car, go to a dealer and deal directly with the Fleet Sales Department as a first choice and the Retail Sales Department as a second choice. If it is a used car you are looking for, follow my recommendations in the following order:

1. Private-party seller.

2. New-car dealer's used-car lot.

3. Rental-company resale lot.

4. Company fleet sales.

5. Independent used-car lot.

6. Bank repossessions.

7. Public auto auctions.

8. IRS and government sales.

Determining the Cost (the Seller's Value)

We will discuss two types of value here:

1. **Dealer new-car cost.**
2. **Used-car "blue book" value.**

Dealer New-Car Cost

The term, *"dealer invoice,"* has become so ambiguous that it really has no bearing on actual dealer cost. There was a time when dealers got an invoice on a new car, and that was what they were required to pay the manufacturer. Then somewhere along the way, someone got the idea of something called "holdback." Holdback is usually a percentage of the dealer invoice price (anywhere from 2% to 5%, sometimes more) which manufacturers hold in reserve and then pay back to dealers at the end of every model year as an incentive to sell out their remaining inventories. So dealers started figuring holdback as part of the vehicle profit. This gave the dealers another 2% to 5% profit on every car. Then came the oil shortage of the 1970s, and in order to stimulate sales, someone else said, "Let's give all of our customers money back if they buy one of our cars." Yes, **rebates**—not just rebates to consumers, but rebates to dealers as well. Every time dealers sold a car, they not only counted on holdback, but if the market was slow they would get money back in the form of dealer incentives (rebates). Over time, this has clouded the issue of the dealer's true cost. In the early 90s, some manufacturers (Chrysler and Toyota, for example) started adding market pricing **adjustment** to the dealer invoice. This did not raise the retail price—only the dealer-invoice amount.

The bottom line is this:

> *The dealer's cost is the amount of the check the dealer sends to the manufacturer to pay for a vehicle when it is sold.*

Often this can be thousands of dollars below the actual dealer invoice. The dealer's total profit in a new car is the difference between the selling price and the dealer's actual cost after deducting all holdback, dealer rebates, and other incentives. When you are negotiating a deal, it is imperative that you remember the differences between **dealer invoice** and **dealer cost.**

Determining dealer invoice is not terribly difficult. There are many fine publications available that will give you complete dealer-invoice figures with which you can tailor your own dealer invoice.

You might think that dealer invoice won't do you much good with all of the extras the dealer may be getting—but believe me, that's not the case. For many years, people have been going into dealerships and paying over-invoice price. Now you just have to go a step further and determine how much the dealer is getting back in incentive and holdback money once a car is sold.

How do you go about this? Start by assuming that the dealer *will* have holdback. Estimate the dealer's holdback at

2.5% of the invoice total. For example, if the dealer invoice on the car you want is $12,485.35, 2.5% of this amount is $312.13. Deducting this amount would reduce dealer cost to $12,173.22. If you negotiate a deal for $400 over invoice, the dealer's profit would in fact be $712.13! The dealer may insist that there is no holdback—which may or may not be true; but assuming there is, the dealer will be put on the defensive and will have to struggle to overcome this hurdle.

The dealer also may have factory-to-dealer rebates. This amount is more difficult to determine because the dealers keep it a closely guarded secret (or they try to). Factory-to-dealer rebates take several forms. When domestic cars are involved, dealer rebates usually are a fixed amount paid to the dealer on each vehicle when it is sold. Import automakers often use a tiered system, in which the amount of the dealer rebate increases as the number of cars sold increases. For example, let's say that when a dealer rebate program starts, the dealer is receiving $500 back on every car sold. As the sales continue and the dealer reaches a certain level, that $500 may become $1,000. Not only could this become $1,000 on all future cars sold; in some incentive programs, the dealer will get the additional $500 on all previous vehicles sold under the program. Many programs have the potential of netting a dealer $100,000 or more in rebate money! You can always ask the dealer how much the incentives are on the car you want—but don't count on the dealer's cooperation. In Step 9, Negotiating the Deal *You Want*, you will learn how to write a purchase commitment based on the dealer's actual cost.

At some point, you may be confronted by a salesperson who tells you that there has been a price increase. Don't panic. Simply tell the salesperson,

> *I understand that from time to time, price increases do occur. I will be more than happy to adjust my figures accordingly when I am shown the dealer invoice.*

Do this in a calm, firm manner to show that you want to be fair and reasonable about the situation.

Do yourself a favor. Do not try to shortcut this step by assuming that the dealer has a certain percentage of markup on the car you want. Many people believe that dealers have 20%, 30%, even 40% markups; and because they believe the markups are this high, buyers often ask for ridiculous discounts which a dealer cannot possibly give. In all fairness, dealers do not have outrageously high markups on their cars. The amount of markup will depend on the model selected; but in general, the markup for entry-level base-model cars is about 11% to 13%, and top-of-the-line models will run 17% to 21% (although some luxury imports will have 20% to 24% markup).

Do your homework when determining dealer invoice/cost, and be sure your information is as accurate as possible.

Used-Car Value

Determining the value of a used car versus the seller's actual cost is going to be a little difficult. Unlike a new car, each used car is unique. Realistically, no two will have the same value. There may be two identically equipped used cars sitting side by side, and their actual values can vary significantly. Value versus seller investment are two completely different terms. The seller's investment can best be described as the total amount of money that a seller has spent to acquire and prepare a car for sale. Normal maintenance costs should not be considered because they are necessary to provide continued operation. The car's value also is in two different figures: the "fair market retail value" and the "wholesale loan value." Let's look first at seller investment.

Regardless of where you are thinking of buying a used car, the seller of that car paid a specific amount in order to acquire it. Whether that seller is the private party who bought the car new or used, the rental-car company who bought the car to rent for a period and then sell, the fleet company who bought twenty of the same cars for employees to drive, or the used-car or new-car dealer who took the car on trade, the car had a value placed on it at the time of purchase. That value, plus any work that is required before selling (such as paint and body work, mechanical repairs for broken parts, and detailing and cleaning), becomes the total seller investment. The seller will determine a selling price based on the current popularity of the specific make and model and the total investment. If a car is exceptionally clean, difficult to find, and in superb condition, the selling price will be much higher. Most private-party sellers don't know how to determine a realistic selling price for their cars, which is why the classified ads show such a wide range of prices for the same year, make, and model of car.

Determining a car's value is far more important than determining the seller's investment. Many sellers may have invested thousands of dollars more in a car than its actual value will ever achieve. I know of one individual who spent over $5,000 restoring a Hillman Minx station wagon that realistically has a value of no more than $2,500 to $3,000 at the most. It is not wise to spend large sums of money restoring obscure cars that the average buyer has never heard of. Just because a seller spends thousands of dollars on a car *does not make it worth the money that seller may ask.*

How do you determine a car's realistic value? This depends upon the type of car you are interested in. Most people are considering later-model used cars, and for this you need to consult one of the major "automotive used car value guides." These manuals are published four to six times a year, and can be found at many public libraries. Lending institutions also have them available because these are the publications they use to determine loan values.

When preparing this newest edition of *Buying Your Next Car*, I contacted the largest publisher of used car value guides, because I wanted permission to use copies of certain pages from their "wholesale guide" to illustrate its proper use in determining car values. I was informed that these types of books are published for the benefit of auto dealers, not buyers. This company, along with another large publisher of value guides, recently issued what they call "consumer editions" for use by the general public. However, I do not recommend purchasing these editions as they do not contain the same information that is made available to dealers, specifically wholesale pricing values, and the retail values they establish do not appear to take into account the collectible desirability of certain nameplates. In fact, the "excellent retail" value shown in one consumer edition is exactly the same as the "suggested retail" shown in their wholesale edition. You can spend $9.95 for one these consumer editions, or you can visit your library or your own bank and borrow their wholesale edition at no charge. The choice is yours.

The layout and concept of used car value guides are basically the same. The books are arranged chronologically by make, model, and year. They list vehicle identification numbers to help you find information on the correct model, and they also may list the manufacturer's original suggested *base* list price. Next they list "base wholesale" and "suggested retail" values. Each model will refer to a different "equipment schedule"—a list of optional equipment and their prices. These equipment schedules usually are listed at the front of the book. On the page opposite the equipment listing, there is usually a mileage chart, which is used to determine an addition to or deduction from the car's value for low or high mileage.

Using the examples in Figures 1 through 4, let's determine the wholesale and retail value for a 1985 Ford Mustang LX Convertible with a standard V6 engine, 82,000 original miles, and the following equipment:

5.0 liter (302) V8 engine option upgrade
5-speed manual transmission
Air conditioning
Cruise control
AM/FM stereo cassette
Aluminum alloy wheels

Figures 1 through 4 are composite pages which are similar to those found in used car value guides. In Figure 1, we find Mustang-V6—Equipment Schedule C, and an entry for LX Convertible. It shows a wholesale price (Whls.) of $4,500 and a suggested retail price (Sug. Ret.) of $6,850. It also shows that for the V8 302 engine, you should add $300 to the wholesale price and $400 to the retail price.

Figure 1

BASE Wholesale value
before adding or deducting
any optional equipment

FORD 1985

Model	ID #	List Price	Wholesale	Retail
MUSTANG 232 V6 Option Schedule C				
"LX" Convert	273	13102	4500	6850
302 V8	M		300	400

SUGGESTED Highest retail
value before adding or deducting
optional equipment

Usually the first 3 to 5
characters of the cars
*V*ehicle *I*dentification
*N*umber or VIN

Amount to ADD or DEDUCT for
a factory installed optional size
engine. If number is in parenthesis ( )
it should be DEDUCTED.

Letter added to VIN
to inducate engine
option installed at
factory

Manufacturers SUGGESTED Base
List price with NO options or transportation

Figure 2

WHOLESALE FACTORY EQUIPMENT 1985

Option	A	B	C	D
Air Conditioning	STD	STD	STD	150
Power Steering	STD	STD	STD	50
AutomatTranssion	STD	STD	STD	150
Stereo Cassette	STD	50	50	25
Power Windows	STD	175	150	100
Power Locks	STD	25	25	25
Tilt Wheel	STD	75	50	25
Cruise Control	STD	25	25	25
Leather Upholstery	300	150	125	75
Sunroof (manual)	N/A	50	25	25
Sunroof (elect)	200	150	125	100
Moonroof	300	200	175	150
T-Tops	300	200	175	150
Wire Wheel Covers	75	50	25	25
Custom/Alloy Wheels	150	125	100	75

DEDUCT FOR:

Option	A	B	C	D
Manual Trans	N/A	(500)	(400)	(250)
Bench Seat	N/A	(75)	(50)	(25)
No Power Strg	N/A	(200)	(150)	(125)
No Air Cond	(400)	(300)	(250)	(175)

Option and/or Excessive Mileage Deductions SHOULD NOT
Exceed 45% of Base Wholesale Value

Figure 3

OPTION MARKUP GUIDE
Use this guide to determine RETAIL value of options

IF WHSLE IS	THEN RETAIL IS	IF WHSLE IS	THEN RETAIL IS
25.00	35.00	500.00	665.00
50.00	65.00	525.00	700.00
75.00	100.00	550.00	750.00
100.00	135.00	575.00	775.00
125.00	165.00	600.00	800.00
150.00	200.00	625.00	835.00
175.00	245.00	650.00	875.00
200.00	275.00	675.00	925.00
225.00	325.00	700.00	965.00
250.00	345.00	725.00	985.00
275.00	375.00	750.00	1025.00
300.00	350.00	775.00	1050.00
325.00	440.00	800.00	1075.00
350.00	450.00	825.00	1135.00
375.00	495.00	850.00	1150.00
400.00	455.00	875.00	1175.00
425.00	555.00	900.00	1210.00
450.00	625.00	925.00	1250.00
475.00	625.00	975.00	1300.00

Figure 4

MILEAGE CHART 1985 MODELS

Miles x 1000	BASE WHOLESALE VALUE				
	0-999	1000-1999	2000-2999	3000-3999	4000-5999
40	125	250	400	550	650
45	125	250	375	475	600
50	100	150	275	450	525
55	75	175	250	400	475
60	75	125	225	300	425
65	50	100	175	250	300
70	25	75	150	175	200
72	25	50	75	100	150
74	25	50	50	100	100
76	0	0	50	50	50
78	0	0	0	0	50
80	25	75	125	150	175
82	50	100	150	200	250
84	100	150	225	275	350
86	125	175	250	325	475

The listing in Figure 1 referred us to Equipment Schedule C. In Figure 2, column C, we locate the optional equipment on our Mustang.

Note this very important fact: The prices in the equipment schedules shown in Figure 2 are **wholesale only.** In the front of the book, "Retail Mark-up" is shown. (See Figure 3.) We used that chart to determine the retail value of the options listed (shown to the right of the wholesale price listed below).

Air Conditioning	STD	STD
Cruise Control	+ 25.W	+ 35 R
AM/FM Stereo Cassette	+ 50.W	+ 65.R
Aluminum Alloy Wheels	+100.W	+135.R
5-speed Manual Trans	−400.W	−455.R

Notice that you must *deduct* for the manual transmission because an automatic transmission is more desirable.

Totaling our figures, we find the Mustang has a "Wholesale" of $4,575 and a "Suggested Retail" of $7,030.

Now we must go to the Mileage Chart (see Figure 4) and check for any allowance or deduction for mileage. First, locate the base wholesale value range at the top of the page. Remember, our Mustang had a "Base Wholesale Value" of $4,500. Find the range from $4,000–$4,999 and follow it downward until the mileage listed in the far-left column is closest to the mileage on the Mustang. In our example, the mileage is 82,000. Where the two intersect is the amount to add or deduct. If the figure you arrive at is in the shaded portion of the chart, *add it.* If the figure is in the white area, *deduct it.* In our example, we must deduct $250 from each of our totals, making the wholesale value of the Mustang $4,325 and the suggested retail value $6,780.

As a general rule, lenders will loan 70 to 80 percent of the wholesale value, which means that our Mustang's loan value would be approximately $3,000 to $3,500. The suggested retail is exactly that—a suggestion of the approximate retail price of this and/or comparable Mustangs with the same equipment. It is important that you figure these as accurately as possible, based upon the equipment, model, and year, in order to achieve an accurate value of the car you are considering.

If you are not considering a recent production-year car, use an "Older Edition" book in a similar way. If you are considering a special-interest, antique or classic car, there are special publications for determining the value of these. It may be in your best interest to get an appraisal from a recognized firm or individual to help establish a value for these types of cars.

Selecting and Test-Driving a Car

Whether you are buying a new or used car, there is always an underlying fear that the car will wind up being a lemon, a piece of junk that you are stuck with. Once you have determined what you are looking for in a car and you have found what appears to be a serious contender, there are steps you must take to assure yourself that you have made the right choice.

First impressions are lasting impressions, and oftentimes they are the car buyer's downfall. A car can look perfect and be a mechanical nightmare. Dealers and private sellers alike know that appearance is the single largest determining factor in selling a car. You need to look beyond the shine and really get underneath the skin of the car you are considering.

To properly evaluate and compare potential cars, get into the habit of doing your evaluations the same way each time with every car. Develop a system and don't deviate, or else you may overlook something really vital. Don't wear really good clothes when test-driving a car because you may get them dirty. If they don't get dirty, you didn't check the car thoroughly.

Your evaluation procedure should be:

1. **Make a general walk-around.**
2. **Road-test the car.**
3. **Get a second opinion.**

The General Walk-Around

This is your first opportunity to examine your potential purchase. Whether you are buying new or used, from a dealer or from a private individual, you need to do this at your own pace and in the way *you* want. The seller may try to direct your attention to various strong points of the car and divert your attention away from weak points and potential problem areas. If this happens, simply advise the seller that you have your own special approach to checking out the car, and then proceed.

Your first area of attention should be the exterior of the car (although most people want to jump inside and get behind the steering wheel). You need to carefully examine the body. Check for any telltale signs of accident damage. Even new cars can receive damage in transit or on the lot, and sometimes it can be extensive. This doesn't mean you should automatically rule out a car that has been in an accident, but it does mean that you should give special attention to any repairs that were made, to be sure they were done properly. If a fender or a hood shows shinier paint than the rest of the car, probably there has been some damage. There is no valid reason to have just part of a car painted. Check corners of fenders and wheel-well openings for signs of plastic body filler used for repairing accident damage. If the car is used, inspect the rocker panel area (this is the area below the doors and between the front and rear wheel-wells) for possible rust-through. If the paint is raised and bubbled underneath, this is a possible sign of serious rust. If you find this, consider passing the car up. Rust in any form can become a serious problem, and the costs of repairing it can be quite high. Rust also can undermine the structural integrity of a car and create possible safety hazards.

If the body appears to be acceptable, open the hood and give the engine compartment the once-over. The things to look for here are soft hoses, worn fan belts, dirty and corroded battery terminals, excessive grease and oil build-up on the engine, loose wires hanging down and unconnected, leaking radiator, mismatched spark-plug wires, and missing or altered emission-control components. This won't be a problem on a new car, but you'd be surprised at the number of little things that are overlooked at the factory and during the initial dealer inspection.

That last item can be extremely important to a potential buyer. First, it is a crime under federal law to alter or remove any emission-control equipment from a motor vehicle. There are severe penalties for doing so. Second, it can be very costly to repair or replace such equipment. If you live in an area that requires annual or semiannual emissions checks, you may be in for a very big surprise if you are not extremely careful. In Step 10, carefully read the section on writing a bill of sale, to see how to protect yourself regarding this.

If the engine compartment appears to be in order, open the trunk and check for a spare tire, jack, and lug wrench. This will also give you an opportunity to look further for rust down in the spare-tire storage area.

While you are examining any part of the car, if the seller tries to distract you or move you to another part of the car, be suspicious!

Next, inspect the interior. Check all door-handle functions, all window controls (either manual or electric), and all instruments and accessories. Any part that doesn't function is a part that either should be replaced before you buy the car or a negotiating point when you are talking price. And if the car is new, wouldn't it be better to have these things taken care of before you take delivery than afterward?

Once you are satisfied that everything on the inside is acceptable, and if you are still seriously interested, you need to move on to the next phase—the road test.

The Road Test

Most people tend to make road tests too short and easy. If you are working with a dealership, the road-test route may be designed to show off the car's best traits—not the worst ones. I am not advocating abusing a car on a road test, but there are certain mandatory considerations you need to make. If at all possible, the engine should be cold and the car should not have been driven for several hours. The reason is simple: Many cars start well once warmed up, but when they are cold they can be very difficult to start. If you have arrived to test-drive a car and it has just been run with no one else looking at it, the seller may be attempting to cover up a hard-start problem.

Make a note of whether the car starts easily or requires a little extra cranking of the starter. Once the engine starts, does it idle smoothly, or is it rough? If it is a little rough, rev the engine slightly but not excessively, and then let your foot off the accelerator and allow the idle to drop back down. Did this make a difference?

With the engine running and the car in park if it is an automatic transmission (or in neutral if it is a stick shift), put on the emergency brake and step out of the car. Walk to the rear and look at the color of any smoke coming out of the exhaust. Black smoke means a rich fuel mixture; gray smoke means burning oil. Some older cars may have a small amount of gray smoke when cold, but this should stop once the car has warmed up. If it doesn't, be cautious.

Next, walk to the front of the car and look at the engine as it idles. Is it smooth, or does it shake badly? Reach up and grab the open hood. How much vibration do you feel? Listen carefully for any unusual tapping or knocking noises coming from within the engine. Also listen for any rumbling exhaust noise which could indicate a leaking exhaust system.

Close the hood and get back into the car. Be sure everyone in the car has a seat belt on before proceeding further. Place the car in gear and proceed on the road test. Do not turn on the stereo except to check its proper operation. You need to be able to hear the car—not music.

If you have to back up to move the car, pay special attention to how smoothly the car shifted from park to the reverse position. Did the transmission clunk, or was it smooth? If the car has a manual transmission, how smoothly did the clutch engage? Once again, when going from reverse into drive, note the smoothness of the shift. Does the car accelerate smoothly and quickly, or does it hesitate and falter? If you are driving an automatic, note the smoothness of the shifts from second to third and into overdrive (if so equipped). If you are testing a manual transmission, be sure to check that the transmission shifts firmly and smoothly without any grinding of gears. Also check to be sure the clutch engages firmly and doesn't slip.

You select the road-test route. Be sure to drive on all types of road surfaces, noting the feel of the car's suspension especially on rougher roads and when cornering. When you apply the brakes, do you feel any pulsation in the brake pedal? This can indicate warped brake rotors or drums. Does the car pull to the left or right when driving? When braking? Does the brake pedal feel firm, or mushy? Find a stretch of road where there is no other car behind you, and try a couple of panic brake stops. *Be sure there are no other cars behind you when you do this, and tell any passengers riding with you what you are going to do before you do it.* In the panic stop, does the car pull sharply in one direction or another? Did you hear any unusual clunking sound from the front end, which might indicate loose front suspension components? Each person considering the purchase should test-drive the car to get the feel of it. This also helps because one person may discover something another person missed.

After returning from the road test, if you are still serious about the car and it is a used car, you need to get a second opinion.

The Second Opinion

This step probably will cost you some money unless you happen to be a mechanic. Any used car you are seriously considering must be taken to a qualified mechanic for further evaluation. To do anything less is asking for trouble. Most repair shops will charge a fee ranging from $25 to $100, depending on how thorough an inspection you want. The Car Evaluation Checklist in the Plan-of-Action Workbook has been designed for a potential buyer and a mechanic to complete. This will help you thoroughly evaluate a car and can clearly determine whether you want to pursue it further.

Remember: A little money spent now may save you hundreds, perhaps thousands, of dollars later. Another point to remember: Any seller who hesitates to allow you to get a second opinion *is not* someone with whom you want to do business.

Negotiating the Deal *You* Want

There are countless books written on the subject of negotiation, and I am not going to try to convince you that this single chapter will cover all of the various facets to negotiation. On the contrary, it is offered only as a guide for the establishment of your game plan.

The one thing that is certain is that new-car and used-car negotiations are different, and negotiating with dealers and private sellers is different. Let's tackle new-car negotiations first.

New-Car Negotiation

For most people, negotiation is the worst part of buying anything. People hate negotiating with dealerships and their personnel because, as a rule, they have no idea of what's going on and whether they are getting a good deal or getting ripped off. Anxiety about the deal is compounded by the notion that dealers would steal from their own mothers.

Nonsense! If you have followed this program carefully and completed your plan of action, you are well prepared. You should have a terrific game plan, and you can feel confident—even a bit excited—about negotiating, secure in the knowledge that you will not ripped off.

You know:

The dealer's plan.
Your monthly payment.
Your qualified interest rate.
How much car you can buy.
What car you want.
The dealer's cost.
The wholesale value of your trade.

If you have been careful, the dealer should have absolutely no idea how you feel about the car, what your budget is, or whether or not you have a trade.

There is one important thing you must understand about negotiations:

> ## Nothing you sign during the negotiations can legally obligate you to purchase a car!

Only by signing a *Finance Contract* or *Cash Purchase Agreement* (which you will do just before taking delivery) can you be obligated to buy a car. *Even then, in most states, unless you physically drive the new car off the dealership premises, you are under no obligation to take the new car.* Even if you have given money to the dealer, physical possession is the key in almost all states. (As with all legal questions, consult your local authorities concerning laws covering this.) Many people foolishly believe that they can take the car and then have three days to change their minds and return it to the dealership. *This is wrong!* Do not believe this for a minute! If, during negotiations, any sales representatives tell you this, demand to have

it *put in writing* and approved and signed by the owner of
the dealership or the general manager. If you ask for this and
there is any hesitation, you can bet that you are being lied
to! Even then, you may wish to consult with an attorney.
Many people have been taken in by this kind of tactic.
Unless you have some written guarantee, do not let dealership personnel talk you into this! In most states, the three-
day Right of Recision (right to change your mind and return
the product) deals only with sales which are solicited and
signed for in the privacy of your home—not in a public place
of business.

Dealers have rights, too, so be sure of your facts and be
prepared to back them up.

Negotiation is really nothing more than a battle of wits—
a game, if you will, that can be both challenging and fun.
Never underestimate your opponent. Sales personnel are
trained professionals who make their living negotiating deals
every day. This does not mean you should feel intimidated.
You are in control. Imagine a game of tug-of-war, with you
at one end and the entire dealership sales force and management team at the other end. You want to pull the dealer to
your side, and the dealer and salespeople want to pull you to
their side. When everyone pulls with the same force and no
one moves, nothing ever happens. Successful negotiations
require **both sides to give, in small amounts,** in order to
reach a point of agreement at some point in the middle (or
in this case, somewhere between full window-sticker price
and dealer cost). Each side wants to be closer to the end of
the rope, and this is where control is vitally important. The
one who maintains control is always the one who walks
away the winner. *Remember, you as the buyer have ultimate control because you can get up and leave at any
time.*

How do you maintain control?

1. *Educate yourself.* (By studying this book and form-
   ing your Plan of Action, you've done this.)
2. *Hide all emotions.*

3. *Maintain a soft, even tone in your voice.* Never raise your voice. Changes in your vocal tone indicate excitement. Never let the dealer hear anything in your voice that could give your feelings away.

4. *Take charge* as soon as negotiations begin. Don't let the dealer start, because that starting price is *full window-sticker* price. You **must** take charge because that will throw the sales personnel off balance. They don't expect it.

5. *Remain firm* in your negotiations. When you raise your offer, do so in very small amounts—$25 at a time. You must be stronger than the dealer, and you must be willing to get up and walk out, no matter how much you want the car. *Remember, there will be other cars at other dealerships.* Sales personnel know this today more than ever, and they know they have only one chance to sell you a car.

6. No matter what happens, **remain calm.** Calm means control, and control means you win.

The more opportunity you have to use your plan of action, the better you will become at negotiating. Remember one important thing, there is a big difference between being firm and being rude. You can maintain control and fulfill your objectives without being rude—and, in fact, you will accomplish far more. By being diplomatic, courteous, and polite, not only will you have a definite advantage, it will drive the dealership sales team crazy! If you maintain your cool, they won't know what to think or how to respond or in which direction to try to take negotiations. They will be totally off balance.

There are basically five types of negotiation:

Four-square.

Payment.

Difference.

Discount.

Over-invoice/Cost.

You ***never*** want to use any of the first four methods, because they favor the dealer and will only cost you money. Why?

Four-square negotiation is designed to confuse customers and keep them off balance.

There should be no ***payment*** to be negotiated, because you have established your payment budget and this isn't going to change.

There should never be a ***difference*** to negotiate, because the dealer shouldn't know you have a trade.

There should never be a ***discount,*** because that means you are starting at full window-sticker and trying to talk the dealer down. You want to start at cost and let the dealer talk you up!

A closer look at each method will show you what is going to happen.

FOUR-SQUARE NEGOTIATION

Many dealers use this type of negotiation because it can be ***very confusing to potential buyers.*** This definitely gives the dealer the advantage. It involves four squares on a worksheet.

The first square is for ***negotiating price.***
The second square is for ***negotiating trade-in.***
The third square is for ***negotiating payment.***
The fourth square is for ***negotiating down payment.***
And all are negotiated at the same time!
This is the ***worst possible scenario for negotiation.*** The dealer wants to keep you confused by throwing all sorts of figures at you and discussing everything at the same time.

From the buyer's standpoint, there shouldn't be any discussion about trade, payment and down payment, because the dealer shouldn't know if you have a trade and the payments and down payments are not negotiable items. Avoid this type of negotiation! If a dealer insists on using it, leave. No good will ever come out of it.

PAYMENT NEGOTIATION

This is the dealers' ***second favorite way*** of selling you a car. If the sales person has done a good job, by this time you are very excited about the possibility of driving home a new car. This will make it very easy for the salesperson to convince you that $20 or $40 a month isn't that much more than you had planned to spend. The salesperson will simply begin negotiations by asking how much monthly payment you had budgeted. Whatever you answer, the salesperson will respond with great dismay that the payment you have in mind is too low for a car of this value. If you persist in not raising your payment, the salesperson probably will write a commitment to buy that will look something like this:

Customer will buy today for payments of
$ _____ per month
X _____

The salesperson then will inquire about how much your down payment will be, and will write it somewhere on the worksheet. Then you will be asked to sign the commitment, showing that you agree to the terms as they are written. Then the salesperson will leave the room to take the commitment to the sales manager.

Notice two very important things about this commitment:

The emphasis is on ***today.*** Time is of the essence. This is a pressure tactic to make you feel obligated to buy right now.

There is absolutely no mention of how long the payments will continue! Your entire game plan may be based on 36-month or 48-month financing, and the salesperson doesn't know this. The sales manager may look at the commitment and find that the payment is fine for 60 months—but that isn't what you want!

The salesperson will return, appearing very happy, and say something like,

> *It looks like we have a great deal for you. You can have this car for the payments you want with only $6,500 down. Isn't that fantastic?*

No, it isn't fantastic. You told them only $3,000 down! The point is, the dealer is saying you can have any payments you want as long as you put down the money the dealer wants. Dealers **always** use full window-sticker price when they start to figure payment negotiations. They simply figure out how much down payment will be required to reach your payment level and still give the dealer a full-price deal. Then they send the salesperson back to give you the "good news." But, using your game plan, you have chosen a car that will fit your payments and your down payment based on the dealer's cost and the amount of markup you have chosen to offer. You know you can buy this car for what you want.

When the salesperson comes back with ridiculous figures, you may be tempted to ask, "What is the price these payments are based on?" The salesperson may answer,

> Let me assure you, in order to get your payments this low, the manager had to lower the price considerably!

The salesperson has totally avoided your question. This is exactly what sales personnel are trained to do. Avoid this type of negotiation. If you have a solid game plan, **your payment should never be a subject of negotiation.** When payment comes up, simply respond by telling the salesperson that the payments are not important to you. The salesperson will probably respond with something like this:

> What you are telling me is that you don't care how much the payments are as long as you get this car. Is that right?

The salesperson wants to make it sound as if the payments will be much higher than you think. Don't fall for this. Simply answer,

> Don't you worry about the payments unless you plan on making them for me.

Keep the salesperson in the dark during any attempt at payment negotiation. The less information the dealership has, the better. If the salesperson still insists on attempting payment negotiation, train yourself to say,

*Look, I know exactly how much payment I can af-
ford. I also know that the interest rate I qualify for,
along with the down payment I intend to make, will
allow me to purchase this car and give some dealer
a reasonable profit. Your manager should also realize this. If you would like to make this deal, fine. If
not, we both know there is a dealer out there who
will be happy to make this deal. So let's quit playing
around and make this deal, or let me leave so I can
go buy my new car.*

Remember not to be rude when you say this. Simply be
firm, but polite. If your Plan of Action is accurate, your
information will be correct and you can say this with confidence.

When the salesperson relays this information to the
sales manager, one of three things will happen:

The sales manager will know that you have done your
groundwork and that you are right. The sales manager may
send the salesperson back to accept your offer.

or,

The salesperson will be sent back to attempt to negotiate payment one last time.

or,

The sales manager may tell the salesperson that there
is a viable deal but to go back and tell you there is **no way** a
deal can be made. The sales manager is trying to call your
bluff, hoping that you will cave in.

If the salesperson comes back and asks for more money
or tells you there is no way of making a deal, very calmly
say, "Thank you for your time and effort." Then **get up to
leave.** You must be prepared to walk out of the dealership
and **not turn back.** If you hesitate or give any indication
that you still want to talk, the salesperson will know you
really want the car and that you will give in at least a little.
Every little bit you give is more money for the dealer. If you
do this, you have just lost.

The salesperson may stop you and say,

Let me go talk to my manager one last time.

This is usually a prearranged plan, especially when the sales manager knows they have a deal. With today's market getting tighter and tighter for the dealers, they don't want to let any deal get away, no matter how small the profit may be.

If the salesperson stops you from leaving, you probably will have the deal you want. This is the ideal situation that buyers would like to see whenever a salesperson attempts to get them to negotiate payments, but it is unpredictable and cannot always ensure success. Remember three things:

1. *It is your money.*
2. *You are in control.*
3. *You can walk out whenever you want.*

DIFFERENCE NEGOTIATION

Here, the dealer wants to concentrate on anything *but* price. If you have made the mistake of telling the salesperson that you have a trade, the new objective for the salesperson is to determine how much you want for the trade, and then to write a purchase commitment based upon the difference between the full window-sticker price and the amount you want for the trade. For example, let's say that you have selected a car which has a full window-sticker price of $20,850, and you have told the salesperson that you want $5,000 for your trade. The salesperson will calculate the difference between the two figures and write a commitment like this:

> *The customer will buy today for a difference of $15,850 plus tax, license, and documentary fee.*
> X _____

Of course, the mistake was in mentioning the trade. Once the existence of a trade is known, the dealer has the superior negotiating position. *But all may not be lost.* You know the dealer's invoice/cost; and you have three bids on your trade, so you have a good idea of your old car's fair whole-sale trade-in value. If you want to continue, you could make an offer to the dealer based on the following formula:

Dealer Invoice — Trade-In Value + Profit

Basically, this means you will **deduct the fair wholesale trade-in value** from the dealer's invoice cost, then **add the amount of profit** that you want to give the dealer.

Invoice	$17,540
Trade-in	− 5,200
Profit	+ 500
Total	$12,840

Then write a commitment that says,

> *I will buy this car now for a difference of $12,840 plus tax and license.*
> X _____

Notice that there is no mention of the documentary fee in the commitment you wrote. Despite what most dealers will lead you to believe, **a documentary fee is not a governmental fee.** It is nothing more than a charge that the dealer assesses for doing all of your paperwork. It is extra profit. By leaving out the documentary fee, you have introduced another point of negotiation with which to combat the dealer. If the dealer insists that you pay the fee, you can insist that the price be lowered by the amount of the fee. When you write a commitment and leave out the documentary fee, the dealer will not be able to charge it because the entire agreement was predicated on a commitment which did not include it.

The salesperson will take your signed commitment to the sales manager. At this point, the dealership will need to appraise your trade-in. The sales manager or used-car manager will take your car for a drive. He will check the "blue book" to determine the low book loan value, and will deduct for reconditioning, market conditions, and anything else that will be required. The sales manager will then offer a counterproposal, probably showing your trade value at $1,500 to $2,000 lower than you have it. The dealer probably is not aware that you have received bids on your trade already, and assumes that you have no real idea of your trade's value. When the salesperson returns with the counterproposal, the ball is in your court. You can counter the counterproposal and play the game for a while, making the salesperson go back and forth; or you can be up-front with the salesperson and say that you have three different bids from independent dealers. At that point, the dealer will probably tell you that you should sell the trade yourself. The dealer then will return to negotiation without a trade. The dealer is hoping you will believe your trade isn't worth nearly as much as you think it is and you will settle for a lot less, thus giving the dealership more profit.

It is always best not to reveal a trade until you have negotiated the price you want on the new car. Keeping your trade-in a secret until the end will keep money in your pocket.

DISCOUNT NEGOTIATION

It is very common for potential buyers to ask for a discount from the window-sticker price. No matter how much discount you ask for, salespeople are trained to express incredible disbelief at the discount you want.

The problem with discount negotiation is that you are starting at the wrong end of the negotiating spectrum. When customers ask for a discount from the full window-sticker price, they are establishing a precedent in which everything hinges on wearing the dealers down by asking them to lower the prices of their cars.

The asking position is the weakest possible position for negotiation, and it will eventually lose.

If you want to negotiate a discount, then you need to know the dealer invoice amount, and figure the total profit the dealer has, minus any dealer incentive. Add the amount of profit you want to allow the dealer, and then ask for a discount based upon these figures. This isn't the best way, but it can be done.

OVER-INVOICE/COST NEGOTIATION

This is the **only** method you should use when negotiating the price of a car!

Why invoice/cost instead of invoice alone? Because dealer incentives and other factors will affect final dealer cost. Factors such as holdback and dealer-added options can greatly obscure the difference between invoice and cost. Remember, don't buy any dealer-added options!

In any deal, the only thing that matters is

How much profit are you willing to give to the dealer to get the car?

In order to negotiate an over-invoice/cost price, you need to determine how much profit you are willing to allow the dealer. The amount over invoice/cost that you have to pay will depend on:

- *Availability*
- *Popularity*

Don't make the mistake of walking into a dealership and attempting to buy the hottest, most limited-production car on the market for $500 or even $1,000 over invoice/cost. Whenever a car is in great demand, you will pay a heavy price to own one. The manufacturer will ensure a limited supply of popular models in order to keep the demand and the price up.

If you want to own the current "hot car" on the market, you have only two alternatives:

Wait for the supply to increase and demand to cool down.

Bite the bullet and pay through the nose.

But don't believe a car is hot just because the dealers and commercials tell you that it is. If a dealer's lot is loaded with the model you want, other dealers probably have just as many.

You should be able to buy *most* domestic cars for $250 to $500 over final dealer *cost* and *most* imports for $250 to $700 over final dealer *cost.* Though $700 may sound high, remember dealer posture. Japanese manufacturers know that their cars are in great demand and will hold out for higher profits—especially the Japanese "Big Three"—Honda, Toyota, and Nissan. Many other quality Japanese cars are easier to buy at more reasonable prices, and you should look closely at these cars. In many cases, the lesser-known nameplates will be as good or better values for the money.

When negotiating an over-invoice/cost price, it is important that you establish control immediately. Once you are inside the office, the salesperson will take out a pad of worksheets (called Sales Order Forms or Customer Proposals) and ask for your name, address, and phone number. The salesperson is starting to take control by getting you to answer questions. This is *not* what you want. Take control by being totally cooperative, even volunteering information before the salesperson asks for it. The salesperson will assume that you really want the car, and will be thrown off balance. Offer to fill out the form "for" the salesperson. While filling it out, casually mention that you have filled out these forms at other dealerships. This will alert the salesperson to the fact that you are shopping for your deal. You are now planting your own "seed of doubt" in the salesperson's mind.

Now it is time to *really* take command. You must start the negotiation process. Ask the salesperson to hand you the worksheet. Tell the salesperson that you are prepared to make an offer. Start the negotiation by ***immediately giving the salesperson a written commitment*** to purchase the car. By doing this, **you *establish the point from which all further negotiations will proceed*.**

The first commitment you write must read exactly like this:

> *I (or we) will buy this car right now for $250 over*
> *dealer invoice, less any rebates and dealer incen-*
> *tives. I (or we) will pay sales tax and license but*
> *no documentary fee.*
> X _____

This written commitment establishes the negotiations from
a point just over dealer cost, and establishes a second negotiation point—that of documentary fee payment. The salesperson may refuse to work with this commitment, and will
attempt to regain control of the negotiations by saying something like,

> *I am not even going to take this to the manager.*
> *He would throw me out of his office. You can't*
> *be serious!*

Look the salesperson in the eye and say very calmly and
slowly,

> *I know you are not permitted to make a decision*
> *like this, so I will write you a check for $500 to take*
> *with you to show your manager I am sincere.*

Get out your checkbook and write a check. The salesperson
may attempt to stop you, but be firm. Tell the salesperson,

> *This is a solid offer. If you don't want to take it to*
> *the sales manager, ask the sales manager to step out*
> *here and I will present it personally.*

Eventually, the salesperson will have to take your offer to
the sales manager. If the salesperson refuses, ask to speak
with the person in charge, and tell that person you want to
make an offer but the salesperson refuses to present it. Sooner
or later, the sales manager will have to look at your offer
and either send the salesperson back with a counteroffer
that will be very close to full window-sticker, or with in-
structions to tell you that you will have to do much better.
   When this happens, calmly say,

> *I feel this is a very fair offer, based on current mar-*
> *ket conditions and vehicle supply. If your manager*
> *feels it is too low, how close is he prepared to come?*

If the manager has made a written counterproposal, the salesperson probably will point to it and say, "This is it." Tell the salesperson,

> *Not good enough. I will make no more offers*
> *until your sales manager comes much closer to*
> *my first offer.*

Or you might choose to say,

> *Very well. Let me see that.*

Take back the worksheet, scratch out your original offer, and rewrite it, adding $25 for a total of $275. Then sign it, hand it back to the salesperson and say,

> *You are going to get very tired going back and forth.*
> *You and I both know that this is a very fair offer for*
> *this car, and if your sales manager isn't willing to*
> *make this deal, another sales manager at another*
> *dealership will.*

The purpose here is to make the dealer give more than the customer. Dealers will give more because they know there are other dealers who *will* sell the same car for $275 over dealer cost. Today's market is flooded, and no manager will refuse a good deal.

When the salesperson returns again from the manager's office, listen carefully, because the sales manager has coached him in exactly what to say. After the salesperson has made his little speech, you say,

> *Now that you've told me what the manager wanted*
> *you to say, what do you want to tell me?*

This tells the salesperson that you are very aware of what is going on behind the scenes.

The entire purpose of negotiation is to meet somewhere at a point where the dealer will accept your offer. By increasing your offer by only $25 each time, the salesperson will have to make ten trips back and forth just to raise your offer $250! Once you, the customer, reach the point at which you do not wish to increase your offer any further, you need to make it clear that time is running out. Tell the salesperson,

> *I will make this offer one last time. If the sales manager doesn't want to accept it, that is okay. Just let me know, and I will go elsewhere to buy my new car. But understand this—I am going to buy a new car today!*

The salesperson will relay the message to the sales manager, who probably will send the salesperson back to try to get you to pay a little more money. ***Don't do it!***

Once you have told the salesperson you are making a last offer, **you cannot change your mind.** Simply say, "Thank you for your time," and get up to leave. The salesperson may make one last attempt to get even $10 from you. *No!* Tell the salesperson, "I have given you every opportunity to make a deal, and if the sales manager doesn't want to make it, that is fine. But I must leave now, because I need to go to another dealer." As you prepare to leave, the salesperson probably will ask you to wait for just a moment while he goes back to speak with the sales manager one last time. After investing this much time, the salesperson ***wants to make this deal.*** Salespeople work long and hard to earn your business, and if they know that there is a deal, they will do anything they can to get it before you leave, because you won't be back. In fact, the sales manager probably has already instructed the salesperson not to let you leave, because there is a deal. If the salesperson does come back and tell you that you have made a deal, thank him and take a seat.

Now you need to ask for complete disclosure of the figures to be sure there has been no misunderstanding. The disclosure should look something like this:

Dealer Invoice		$13,548
Agreed Markup	+	275
Dealer Incentive	−	1,000
Customer Incentive	−	1,000
Subtotal		$11,823
Sales Tax		000 (Add your state's rate)
License Fee		000 (Add your state's rate)
Total Sale Price		$11,823

The figures may not appear in this order, but they should be clearly spelled out.

A dealer who has made a deal in good faith should not be surprised when you ask to see verification of the current incentive program and rebate program, as well as a copy of the actual dealer invoice. A dealer who hesitates to show you this information is hiding something. If you are not comfortable with what you are hearing, remember that you can leave anytime.

Be sure the dealer hasn't added a documentary fee into the figures. If he has, simply point out the "error" and ask to have it removed.

The sales manager may tell you that he will show you copies of all incentive and rebate programs when you are in the finance office to sign your paperwork. This is fine, as long as you are given an opportunity to examine them carefully and are not rushed. *You must be satisfied that the figures are accurate before you sign anything.*

If you are satisfied that everything is in order, you can make arrangements to take delivery. If you do have a trade-in, now is the time to introduce it into the deal. Simply tell the sales manager that you have a trade-in and you would like to have it appraised. Assure the manager that you have every intention of buying the new car. Let him know that you already have three appraisals, and if his appraisal is close, you will let him have the car. Say,

> *If your appraisal is quite a bit lower, I will take my trade and sell it to one of the other appraisers, and then I will return and buy the new car.*

The sales manager won't want you to do this because the whole deal could be lost. The sales manager may ask to see the appraisals you already have. Show them, so the dealer knows where he has to be in order to make the deal now. As long as the appraisals are in line, the dealer probably will match one of them. Even if the dealer's appraisal is $50 to $100 less, it may be better for you to take the deal rather than having to go sell your car and then go back to the dealership. If the dealer's appraisal is far below the others, tell him that delivery of the new car will have to wait until you have time to sell your trade to one of the other appraisers. Offer to give the dealer a deposit, and set up a time to return and take delivery. There is still a good chance that the dealer will match one of the other appraisals because he wants you to take delivery of the new car *now!*

Used-Car Negotiation

Why is there a difference in negotiation for a used car? Because unlike new cars, each and every used car is unique. No two cars are cared for the same way, driven the same way, or have exactly the same mileage. Five used cars of the same make and model may have considerable difference in their "blue book" values, depending upon mileage and condition. Popularity or desirability also plays a large part in how you will negotiate for a used car.

You can't determine a seller's cost as closely, because you don't know what has been done to a car. The only guide is the value you determine by using a "blue book". Since this is exactly what a lender is going to do, it probably is a good place to start.

A dealer's approach to negotiation is going to be basically the same as if you were dealing on a new car. The salesperson will try to close you on payments or maybe use the four-square plan, but what you need to do is simply this:

Based upon the "blue book" figures you obtain, determine how much over the wholesale price (or under, if the car is one of several of the same year and

model with similar equipment) you are willing to pay.
Then deduct $100 to $200 so the dealer will be able to
talk you up in price a little bit.

When you make your offer, realize that you probably
will wind up somewhere between "blue book" wholesale and
suggested retail. However, by starting below wholesale, you
have the advantage. Take control just as if you were buying a
new car. Make the first move, and make the dealer do the
asking for more instead of you asking for less. The proposal
you write for the salesperson should look like this:

> *I/We are prepared to purchase this car right now for*
> *(the amount you have decided upon) plus sales tax*
> *and license but no documentation fee.*
> X _____

The salesperson probably will try to plant a substantial seed
of doubt:

> *This is the nicest used car on the lot. You must be*
> *kidding. There is no way we are going to sell this car*
> *for that low price.*

Your response will be simple:

> *How close are you prepared to come?*

The salesperson will respond with something like,

> *The price that is on the window is our best price—*
> *but maybe I can get the manager to knock off a cou-*
> *ple of hundred dollars.*

Many of these statements and responses will be the same as
in new-car negotiation. It all comes down to who has the
most strength and stamina, and who can hold out the long-
est and give up the least amount of money. The key is to
maintain control. Once you have reached a point where you
don't wish to go further, simply tell the salesperson,

> *This is a fair offer. I am going to buy a car today,*
> *and if it isn't here, I have several other choices. My*
> *last offer was my final offer. Will your manager ac-*
> *cept it, or not?*

You **must** be willing to stand by this statement. Remember, there **will** be other cars, and you will be able to get close to the price you want if you are **reasonable** and well prepared.

Your next move is to wait. Don't say anything. If the salesperson comes back with a counteroffer, get up to leave, because you said it was your final offer. You cannot deviate from that position, or you lose your credibility and control.

Use your judgment carefully, and plan your approach thoroughly. Know what the dealer has, know what it's worth realistically, and be fair in your offer. But remember to start low, and make the dealer do the work. If you do it right, you'll have fun, too!

Buying from private-party sellers is different still, because basically they have only one or two cars to sell. If they have advertised properly, they will have a large pool of potential customers to choose from. Private sellers whose ads state that their price is firm are either crazy, or they know that they will easily get the price they are asking. In this case, you have two choices:

Pay the price

or

Keep on looking.

Once again, if you have done your homework, you will know whether these sellers are being realistic, or just think they have something worth the money. If they are getting a lot of traffic on the car, odds are that they will get their price. If they are getting very little traffic, they probably overestimated the car's desirability. One thing is certain: If you tell them you are prepared to pay a specific amount **right now,** even though your offer is less than their firm price, they may well accept it.

Sellers who have named a price or said "Best offer" have clearly indicated that they are negotiable. You need to determine where you stand on the car and know its value so you can make an objective offer that will meet your requirements and make the seller happy.

Many of the same commitments to buy that you can use with dealers will work when you deal with private sellers. Tell them that you are prepared to buy today, and that there are other cars like theirs out there. If they have checked their ads in the newspaper, they may have seen four or five other models like theirs, some of which may have been priced well below theirs. This fact definitely puts them under pressure. If potential buyers walk away when there are several other cars just alike for sale, the odds are that they won't be back. The private-party sellers usually have only one car to sell, and if they chase away all the customers by being unreasonable, sooner or later they realize that they have acted in haste. Once you have made an offer, give these sellers your phone number and tell them that you would still be interested if they don't get any better offers. Often, this works out for a buyer. Private-party sellers seldom are polished salespeople. Remember, **prepare** and **be in control.** There will be another car out there somewhere. Negotiate smart, not hard—and you'll get what you want.

Completing the Paperwork

Paperwork is the single most important aspect of *any* financial purchase. More headaches and ripoffs are caused by failure to carefully examine any and all documentation regarding the purchase than at any other time during ownership. New or used, cash deal or financed, it makes no difference. Once negotiations are concluded, close and careful scrutiny of *all* paperwork involved, and the ability to write and execute a Bill of Sale if you are buying from a private individual, are the top priorities.

Let's first look at purchases through dealerships.

Dealership Sales Paperwork

Here is a list of the most likely paperwork a new car buyer will face:

- **Finance Contract** (if financing through a dealer) or
- **Purchase Agreement** (if paying cash or financing through your bank, credit union or other source).
- **Promissory Note** from you to the Dealer (if you are going to be making a deferred down payment later).
- **State Department of Motor Vehicle Documents.**
- **Power of Attorney.** (This allows the dealer to take care of your vehicle licensing for you.)
- **Warranty Registration Book** (if you are buying a new or late-model used car with factory warranty remaining).
- **Extended Warranty Registration** (if applicable).
- **Federal Warranty Notification Sticker** (on used cars).
- **Promissory Note or "Due Bill"** from the dealer for work or equipment to be provided *after* you take delivery.
- **Customer Satisfaction Questionnaire.** (This may or may not be something a dealer asks you to complete. It is not of substantial importance.)

State laws and Department of Motor Vehicle regulations will vary, so you may have more or fewer documents than this. Check each document carefully. Let's take a closer look at each one.

FINANCE CONTRACT AND/OR PURCHASE AGREEMENT

These two documents are essentially the same, and the dealer may even use the same form.

The first and most important rule is:

> *Never sign any purchase or finance contract until you examine it very carefully.*

This cannot be stressed enough. During the excitement created when buying a new car, once all the negotiations are finished, many people will relax, let down their guard, and make a fatal mistake by just signing paperwork without examining it. If you do this with your finance contract, you may cost yourself a great deal of money.

The primary component of a finance/purchase agreement is a ***description of the vehicle purchased.*** This includes a listing of the ***vehicle identification number. Compare this with the car you selected and negotiated.*** Dealers have been known to switch cars to one with just a few less options, or perhaps to one that had been damaged and repaired but is still the same color and trim. You may suddenly notice that the car you drive home doesn't have cruise control. When you bring it to the dealer's attention you may hear,

> *That wasn't on the car you negotiated for; it must have been on another one you looked at!*

Double-check the vehicle identification number when you choose the car, before you negotiate for it, and before you sign any kind of contract to purchase it.

The items the dealer adds to the basic contract are:

- A list of agreed-to options that may have been added.
- The sale price of the car.
- If financing through the dealer, the interest rate, finance charge, total of all payments, the first payment due date.
- Applicable sales tax.
- License fees.
- Documentary fee (if you let him).
- State filing fees (if applicable in your state).
- Extended warranty price and description (if applicable).

There also will be all of the printed documentation outlining various contract clauses, such as your obligations to the lender, what happens if you fail to meet those obligations, and the lender's rights under the contract.

Be sure you examine your purchase agreement and/or finance contract very carefully. Compare the figures you agreed upon during negotiations with those in the contract. Be certain they have not been changed and that nothing has been added (for example, extended warranty or contract insurance). Many dealers will attempt to "sneak" things into a contract. If you don't notice them, you are fully obligated to take them once you sign the contract and accept delivery. Never let the finance manager leave the office with a signed contract unless you are given a copy first! It is very easy for a contract to be altered after it has been signed if all of the copies are intact.

PROMISSORY NOTE FROM BUYER TO LENDER

This is not uncommon when dealers arrange financing. Many manufacturers have their own lending institutions, such as General Motors Acceptance Corporation or Ford Motor Credit. If you do not have all of your down payment up front, many of these lenders (and sometimes some banking institutions) will give you time (usually 30 to 45 days maximum) to acquire the remaining amount. This is called a *deferred payment* and is a lump-sum payment. The terms may be spelled out on the finance contract, or they may be in the form of a separate promissory note which will be signed by both parties. This is not something to enter into lightly, because it may mean that if you don't come up with the additional down payment *as well as your regular agreed-upon monthly payment,* you will have to return the car. Be sure you can afford to enter this kind of agreement.

STATE DEPARTMENT OF MOTOR VEHICLES DOCUMENTS

These are your vehicle registration forms. Check them over very carefully to be sure of the following points, because this information will be transferred to the title or other ownership document:

- Correct spelling of all names that will appear on the title, and the correct legal use of the terms **and** or **or.** These terms can be very important because when there is more than one registered owner of a car, in *most* states the use of the word **and** between the names (such as Joseph **and** Ruth) legally means that **both individuals' signatures are required in order to sell the car;** but if the word **or** is used such as Joseph **or** Ruth), then only one person's signature is required to sell the car.

Note: I refer to a title when speaking of an ownership document; however, not all states are "title states." As a rule, a title is a document which requires the seal of a licensed or registered notary public to witness any signatures. Some states provide only "Certificates of Ownership." These documents may not require a notary. Be sure you are aware of your state's requirements and the type of documents it issues.

- Correct vehicle identification number.

- Correct mileage (especially if a used car).

- Registered lien holder. (This is the lender or finance company.) This document prevents people from selling cars that are financed without paying them off first.

POWER OF ATTORNEY

This is required by some states in order for the dealer to take care of all of your registration with the Department of Motor Vehicles. It is limited in use and is not used for any purpose other than to save you a trip to the license bureau.

WARRANTY REGISTRATION BOOK

A new or late-model used car comes with either a full factory warranty or the remainder of the factory warranty, depending on the car's age and mileage. If it is a new car, you should receive a Warranty Registration Book which is filled out with your name, address, the vehicle identification number, date of purchase, mileage at time of purchase, and name of the dealership from which the car is purchased. This information will be required to show proof of warranty and to avoid having to pay for repairs. *Be sure that the mileage shown in this book is correct, or it will affect the duration of warranty.* With a new-car purchase, your warranty should start from the day you take delivery regardless of how many miles are on it. For example, if you buy a demonstrator that has 3,000 miles on it, your warranty should start at 3,001 miles and run for the manufacturer's full warranty period. This ensures that you are not short-changed on warranty coverage.

EXTENDED WARRANTY REGISTRATION

If you are purchasing an extended warranty, this will serve as the document that not only extends the warranty coverage but also will be used to eliminate or reduce any deductible which may have existed in the standard factory warranty. Be very sure that the duration and terms of the warranty are the same as you agreed to in negotiation. Some dealers will substitute a shorter-term warranty with less coverage, and if you don't notice it, you are stuck with the situation.

FEDERAL WARRANTY NOTIFICATION

This is required on *all used cars* sold by a licensed car dealer. This document requires the dealer to state in writing and post clearly on the window of any used car the extent of any warranty offered on the car. The form is a two-part carbon form. The buyer signs and keeps one form at the time of delivery; the dealer keeps the other copy on file. This provides warranty protection for the consumer. Bear in mind this does not require the dealer to put a warranty on a used car; it requires the dealer only to state what warranty, if any, has been put on it.

Many people fail to pay close attention to this document when they are negotiating for a car. If you do not take delivery at that moment but intend to come back, remember that you won't get a copy of this form until you sign your paperwork and take delivery. If you leave, the dealer has the opportunity to remove that form and replace it with another form showing less or even no warranty. *Protect yourself.* If you intend to come back later to do the paperwork and take delivery, demand a photocopy of this document before you leave.

PROMISSORY NOTE OR "DUE BILL" FROM THE DEALER

This is a binding document which lists anything the dealer promises to do for you after you have signed all paperwork and taken delivery of the car. *Never* accept a dealer's word that "We will take care of it for you." You will be surprised at how short the dealer's memory becomes after you drive away from the lot.

CUSTOMER SATISFACTION QUESTIONNAIRE

Most dealerships may have your salesperson complete this form for you. In recent years, manufacturers have become aware of how important customer satisfaction is, and they ask for information in order to evaluate your feeling about the dealership and the products that are being sold.

SMOG AND/OR SAFETY INSPECTION CERTIFICATE

Not all states require this inspection certificate. In most states, licensed dealers are required to provide this information. The inspection will usually be done before you take delivery, so there is a chance that you will not see specific documentation concerning it. If you are unsure, check with your local authorities and ask the dealer to see any compliance forms that the state may require.

Private-Party Sales Paperwork

The paperwork required when you buy from a private party, although not as extensive, is no less important for your protection. As a buyer, you have the right to expect a seller to stand behind any claims made. Private parties selling cars are not exempt from the laws concerning false and misleading statements made during the sale of a car; but you must be sure that the documentation you receive from the seller clearly spells out any claims made to entice you to buy. This includes any printed statements made in any published advertisement. You must have documentation for the following:

- Copy of the advertisement placed to sell the car.
- Bill of Sale from the legal owner to you. This bill of sale *must* outline any claims made by the seller for which you may legally hold the seller liable.
- Clear proof of ownership from the seller.
- Proof of current valid registration.
- Smog and/or Safety Inspection Certificate
- Receipts and/or Proof of Warranty for any transferable warranty items on the car.

Let's look more closely at each item.

COPY OF ADVERTISEMENT USED TO SELL THE CAR

The wording of an advertisement may become very important in a small-claims court case. If you claim that the ad said one thing and the person who sold the car denies it, nothing will speak better for you than the actual page from the newspaper. (I mean, the entire page showing the date at the top.)

BILL OF SALE

This is the single most important document you will execute when buying from a private party. This form, if properly written, will afford you all of the necessary protection and grounds for legal recourse that may become necessary if you feel that you have been misled and defrauded by the seller. A Bill of Sale must be very explicit, citing in writing any specific claims that a seller has made as to condition and repairs that have been recently performed. No small-claims court will decide in your favor unless you can provide substantial documentation to back up your claims. The old saying, "Let the buyer beware," is true. If you fail to beware, there is **nothing you can do** because private-party sellers are not licensed or bound by the state. Any claim against a private party must be a civil claim in a civil court; it is your word against the seller's unless you can prove in writing that a seller has made false claims in order to sell the car.

Below is a sample of a Bill of sale that protects **both** buyer and seller:

I, _____ (seller's name) _____ , for value received in the amount of $_____ (written amount here) _____, do hereby sell and convey to _____ (buyer's name) _____ the following described vehicle:

___ (year) ___ (make) ___ (model) _____(vehicle identification number)

Seller further states that (he/she) is the sole legal owner of the above-described vehicle; and further states that said vehicle meets all applicable federal and state safety and emission requirements that were in effect when vehicle was manufactured, and that such equipment is fully functional as intended. Seller further warrants that all State Department of Motor Vehicles license and registration fees are current; and that there are no outstanding citations or violations for which the buyer may be compelled to pay penalties. Seller has further indicated the following as an enticement for buyer to purchase said vehicle: (Here you must list anything that the seller has indicated was done to the car or has implied concerning the condition of the car.) *Seller makes no other claims, either verbally or in writing, as to the condition of the car. Buyer has had the opportunity to examine and drive said car; and further, has been given the opportunity to have the car examined by an independent facility at (his/her) own expense. Buyer is satisfied with the claims stated above, and understands that no other claims have been made except those stated above. Seller understands that (he/she) can and will, at the buyer's discretion, be held liable for the statements made by the seller in this document. Seller further agrees that, should legal action be required to enforce such claims, the seller shall be liable for any and all court costs incurred.*

Dated this _____ *day of* _____*19* _____
Seller: _____
Buyer: _____
Witness or Notary: _____

A seller who made claims in good faith should not have any problem signing such a document, provided that everything has been clearly spelled out. If a seller has made extensive claims about the condition of the car and does not want to sign such a document, you can assume that the seller is being less than truthful. Forget the whole deal.

CLEAR PROOF OF OWNERSHIP

The seller must provide the buyer with either a notarized title or a certificate of ownership (if not in a title only-state). The name of the individual selling the car should be ***clearly*** and ***visibly listed*** on the front of the document. If any other person's name is listed, there may be a problem. The person listed on the front is the ***legal owner*** and the ***only*** person authorized to sell the car. If there is a different name listed the person selling the car should either provide you with a Power of Attorney or some other recognized legal document authorizing that person to sell the car. Also, there should be ***no lien holder listed.*** If there is one, there ***MUST*** be a Release of Lien provided. This is a document provided by a lender when a loan is paid off and a lien is no longer legally valid. Some documents will have a place where the lender can sign off and release the lien, while other documents may have a separate document showing the release. In any case, *Never give any person selling a car any money if there is a lien and the person cannot prove that the lien is paid off, making the car free and clear.*

PROOF OF CURRENT REGISTRATION

This is important unless you are buying a project car to restore in your spare time. Most states require current registration be paid at the time ownership is transferred. If you buy a car that doesn't have current registration tags, you may be held liable for any past-due license fees, traffic fines, or other legal obligations filed against the car. If you don't have proof of current registration, make the seller go with you to the Department of Motor Vehicles to pay the bills if there is a problem.

SMOG AND/OR SAFETY INSPECTION CERTIFICATE

Most states require that the seller obtain any required certificate of this nature before selling a car. *It is the seller's responsibility.* Accepting a car without proof of compliance in these areas can cost you hundreds—even thousands—of dollars in repairs. If you have not protected yourself with a bullet-proof Bill of Sale, you are stuck for the repairs.

RECEIPTS AND/OR PROOF OF WARRANTY

Any time the seller has indicated that repairs were made that have a warranty, you need to do two things. First, check to see if the warranty is transferable. (In most cases, they are not.) Second, if it is transferable, be sure to get the documentation, because without it you have no warranty.

This may seem like a lot of work, but it is the only way to clearly protect yourself when buying from any seller who is not a licensed automobile dealer. The Plan-of-Action Workbook includes a Bill of Sale form, and there are checklists for you to be sure you have all necessary documentation. Use them to avoid any potential problems.

Remember, any seller who is not willing to back up in writing the claims made, whether in an advertisement or verbally, is not someone you want to do business with. If you choose to go ahead under such circumstances, you will have yourself to blame if problems arise.

Taking Delivery

There are three rules for taking delivery:

Never take delivery after dark.

Never take delivery on a rainy day.

Never take delivery of a dirty car.

All of these circumstances do one thing:

They hide flaws!

If you are buying from a dealer, you must examine your car before you sign any paperwork. You need a chance to re-check the vehicle identification number and see if everything the dealer promised to do has been done.

If you are buying from a private seller, you need a chance to see that everything that was on the car—including stereo equipment—is still on the car. (Sometimes a private seller will show a car with a really nice expensive sound system; and the after the deal is made but before you take delivery, will substitute another system that looks similar but is of poorer quality.)

Check just as carefully as you did when you were going for a test drive. If all work promised has been performed and the car meets your approval, then—*and only then*—you can do the paperwork. If things are not as they should be, simply tell the seller that when everything is done as agreed, you will consummate the deal. If the seller tells you that some of the work will have to be done later, *get it in writing*. Have the seller list not only *what* is to be done, but *when* it is to be done. No exceptions!

If you do everything as outlined in this book, you will be able to take delivery of your car knowing that you have maintained control, negotiated a good deal, and gotten a good product. After all, that's what we all want—and what we are entitled to.

Should You Lease?

Somewhere on your journey to car ownership, some salesperson will attempt to convince you that in order to afford the car you desire, leasing is the only practical alternative. This probably will happen if the dealer has attempted to close you on monthly payments and has not been able to get you to increase the amount you have set. The salesperson may tell you,

> *If you lease, we can come much closer to the payment you would like to have.*

This may be true, but most people do not understand that:

Leasing is nothing more than long-term rental.

Leasing is also a gold mine for dealers, at the expense of buyers.

Before you consider leasing, read this chapter very carefully. Laws concerning leasing may vary widely from one state to another, so be sure to check applicable leasing laws within your own state.

When you lease a car, you are merely renting it back from a leasing company that purchased it from a dealer.

Leasing contracts are made for a specified period of time, usually 24, 36, 48, or 60 months (although some companies will arrange leases on high-priced exotic cars for up to 10 years).

Just who should consider leasing?

- Businesses seeking possible tax advantages.
- People who keep their cars for only a few years.
- People who don't want to own a car.

Just who should not consider leasing?

- People who keep cars for a long time.
- People who put high mileage on their cars.

When you lease a new car, the reason the payments will be lower is that you are paying for only a portion of that car's total value for a specific period of time. You are paying for the depreciation, or the estimated amount the car's value will decline during the lease period. When you purchase a new car, after all of the payments are made, *you own it.* When you lease a new car, after all of the required lease payments are made, it belongs to the leasing company. You have made payments for a specific period of time; and at the end of that period, all you have to show for it are a pile of cancelled checks and the offer of the leasing company to allow you to lease another car from them. In most cases, if you do wish to purchase the car you have been leasing, the leasing company will allow you the opportunity to purchase the car for its fair market value. (In fact, certain types of leases *require* you to do this.) If you plan on buying the car at the end of the lease, the rule is simple:

Don't lease it! Buy it now!

Leasing negotiations and leasing contracts have many words and terms that may not be familiar to you. The following are some of the more important terms and their definitions. If you are going to consider leasing, you must fully understand these terms and how they can affect you.

Lessee: This is you—the person leasing. You are not a buyer.

Lessor: This is the company you are leasing from. This is **not** the dealer, but the company you will be making payments to.

Closed-end Lease: This is the most common type of lease. It gives you the option of purchasing the car at the end of the lease term for a predetermined amount of money. If you choose not to purchase, you simply return the car to the dealer or lease company, pay a lease termination fee (usually $200 to $500), and end your obligation. *If you must lease, be sure you have a closed-end lease.*

Capitalization Cost (Cap Cost): This is the amount of money the leasing company will pay a dealer to buy the car that you lease. As the lessee, you are never told how much money this might be. Face it, you are not buying the car, so it's none of your business. (At least, this is how most dealers and lease companies look at it.) Most states do not have laws concerning disclosure of the capitalization cost. Not knowing this amount can cost you dearly. *Insist on full disclosure* of this amount.

Residual Value: This is the **predetermined estimated "fair market value" the car will have at the end of the lease term.** This amount will be disclosed before signing the lease, so you will know how much you will be required to pay for the car if you choose to buy it at the end of the lease term. Depending upon the term, the type of car, and other factors such as popularity and availability, the residual value may be anywhere from 18% to 60% of the original window-sticker price.

Cap Reduction: This is just another way of saying "down payment." Most leases do not require a specific down payment, but they do require "up-front costs." The cap reduction reduces the capitalization cost and thereby reduces the amount of the monthly payment. No matter what you call this, the end result is the same.

Money Factor: Leasing companies never use the words "interest rate." A money factor is the interest rate used to compute your monthly lease payment. As the money factor goes up, so does the payment. As the money factor goes down, so does the payment. Sounds a great deal like interest rate, doesn't it? This is another item that is never disclosed.

Let's recap this situation so far. We are renting a car that we don't know the price of, at an interest rate (money factor) the lease company doesn't have to disclose. Having fun yet?

Up-Front Costs: These are initial costs you pay when taking delivery. They usually consist of:

- The first monthly lease payment.
- A security deposit equal to one payment.
- First year's license and registration fees.

Tax: This is sales tax paid on each monthly payment. When purchasing a car, you pay sales tax on the full purchase price; but when leasing, you will never own the vehicle, so you cannot be taxed on its full purchase price.

Mileage Penalty: Sounds nasty, doesn't it? Well. it is. All leases, regardless of the term, are written with a clause limiting the number of miles you may drive. This is normally 1,250 miles per month or 15,000 miles per year. Lease companies consider this to be the normal mileage that cars will be driven. Given this limitation, a car on a 5-year lease has a total allowance of 75,000 miles. The mileage penalty is the amount of money per mile that the leasing company charges for every mile driven over the limit. These penalties usually range from 5 to 20 cents per mile. This may not sound like much, but let's assume that you drive 15,000 miles over the limit and you are charged a penalty of 12 cents per mile. This would mean that when you return the car to the leasing company, you would have to pay a penalty of *$1,800!* The only way to avoid this penalty is to be sure you don't exceed the mileage limitations or that you purchase the car at the end of the lease period. Some dealers and leasing companies will tell you that if you know you will exceed the allowable mileage limit, you should increase the mileage limit in the lease terms. If you do this, the payment can skyrocket. Be very careful about mileage penalties.

Normal Wear and Tear: Lease companies reserve the right to charge you for any unusual wear and damage which might occur while their car is in your possession. And who defines normal wear and tear? Why, the lease company, of course! You should ask and expect to receive a clearly-defined statement of exactly what the leasing company defines as Normal Wear and Tear.

There are two things concerning leasing which are often used by salespeople to entice you to lease—*and both are total lies!*

First, they will tell you that is it *easy* to get out of a lease early (before the scheduled termination date). *Never believe this.* When you lease, you have a **binding agreement** with the lease company to keep the car for a specific period of time. If you want to get out of the lease early, most lease companies require that the lease be **paid off in full, including the residual.**

If you were buying a new car and financing it, you could pay off your loan early and get a refund on the unused portion of the lender's finance charges. Most leasing companies compute a lease payoff by totaling the remaining payments, adding the residual payment, and then deducting the appraised value. Once this total amount is paid, the car is yours to do with as you please. The entire purpose of leasing was to avoid this, so why allow it to happen? If any salesperson or leasing agent implies that you can terminate a lease at any time without being penalized, ask to see the leasing contract clause regarding early lease termination. If the salesperson hesitates, there is cause to be suspicious.

The second lie is that it is easy to get someone else to assume your lease payments. Forget this, too. Any person assuming a lease must meet all of the leasing company's criteria, and even then, most companies do not want to lease a used car—which is what you are driving.

Don't fall for these lies! They are common tactics used over and over again. If you must lease, *demand* **full disclosure of all terms, and** *get every promise in writing.*

Extended Warranties: Are They Worth the Price?

Whether you should consider an extended warranty depends first on several factors:

1. **Are you buying a new car?**
2. **Are you buying a used car?**
3. **Are you going to keep your car more than four years?**
4. **Are you going to put a lot of miles on the car?**
5. **Do you tend to neglect routine maintenance?**
6. **Do several people drive the car?**

If you can answer yes to any of the above except #1, then an extended warranty probably will be a good investment. If you are buying a new car and an extended warranty will offer you "peace of mind," it may be worth the price of the warranty.

An extended warranty is designed to enhance and prolong the existing warranty coverage that a manufacturer provides. In the case of a used car, it may be the only warranty available. If a new-car warranty calls for a deductible to be paid on warranty repairs, an extended warranty will substantially reduce or eliminate this deductible altogether. An extended warranty on a used car will almost certainly require a deductible to be paid.

Most manufacturers offer substantial basic warranties—many as much as 60,000 miles of bumper-to-bumper coverage. Under these warranties, everything on a car, from the front bumper to the rear bumper and all parts in between, is covered. Tires and batteries may be covered under a separate warranty provided by the tire or battery manufacturers and may not be for the same period of time as the basic car warranty. Some manufacturers also cover normal routine service, such as oil changes.

Before you consider the purchase of an extended warranty, carefully examine the manufacturer's standard warranty. Specifically look at what is covered, how long it is covered, and what is *not* covered. If there is a deductible, is it a single deductible for each visit to the dealer regardless of how many warranty repairs are made during that visit, or is the deductible required for each item of warranty service provided?

Whether an extended warranty is available for a used car depends upon the age and mileage of the car being purchased. A late-model used car may still have some of the original warranty available, and it should be transferable. If you are buying an older used car, you may definitely want to consider an extended warranty, if one is available.

There are two basic types of extended warranties:

• Those offered by a manufacturer.
• Those offered by independent warranty companies.

The important thing to consider is how difficult it is to:

Obtain warranty service.

Get reimbursed if you have to pay for the repair up-front.

Find an "authorized" repair agency.

Transfer the warranty.

Many warranties offered by "independent" companies may require that you get prior authorization or pay for the repair, and then seek reimbursement. If the warranty company chooses to decline the claim, you have no way of recovering the money you spent. The warranty also may not be transferable if you sell your car.

Negotiate the price of an extended warranty just as you negotiated the price of your car. This is a high-profit item, so don't let a dealer push you into buying an extended warranty. Most manufacturer's new-car extended warranties can be purchased any time before the first 12 months or 12,000 miles of ownership. If in doubt, check it out!

Interest-Rate Payment Charts

The following charts provide monthly payment figures within $1.00 of the actual payment as calculated on all finance and lending institution computer systems. The payment amounts have been rounded **up** to the nearest whole dollar to insure that the actual payment will be slightly lower. There will be finance managers who insist that these are not accurate figures. *Don't believe them!*

Remember this rule when considering how long you should finance:

> *The longer the finance term, the more you can finance for the payment you have budgeted*

but:

> *The longer the finance term, the longer it will take to establish equity in your car.*

Interest Rate: 2.9%

Amount you can finance:	Monthly payment amount for:			
	24 months	36 months	48 months	60 months
$ 6,000.00	$ 257.00	$ 174.00	$ 133.00	$ 108.00
6,500.00	279.00	189.00	144.00	117.00
7,000.00	300.00	203.00	155.00	126.00
7,500.00	322.00	218.00	166.00	135.00
8,000.00	343.00	232.00	177.00	144.00
8,500.00	365.00	247.00	188.00	152.00
9,000.00	386.00	261.00	199.00	161.00
9,500.00	407.00	276.00	210.00	170.00
10,000.00	429.00	290.00	221.00	179.00
10,500.00	450.00	305.00	232.00	188.00
11,000.00	472.00	319.00	243.00	197.00
11,500.00	493.00	334.00	254.00	206.00
12,000.00	514.00	348.00	265.00	215.00
12,500.00	536.00	363.00	276.00	224.00
13,000.00	557.00	377.00	287.00	233.00
13,500.00	579.00	392.00	298.00	242.00
14,000.00	600.00	406.00	309.00	251.00
14,500.00	622.00	421.00	320.00	260.00
15,000.00	643.00	435.00	331.00	269.00
15,500.00	664.00	449.00	342.00	278.00
16,000.00	686.00	465.00	354.00	287.00
16,500.00	709.00	480.00	365.00	296.00
17,000.00	730.00	494.00	376.00	305.00
17,500.00	752.00	509.00	387.00	314.00
18,000.00	773.00	523.00	398.00	323.00
18,500.00	795.00	538.00	409.00	332.00
19,000.00	816.00	552.00	420.00	341.00
19,500.00	838.00	567.00	431.00	350.00
20,000.00	859.00	581.00	442.00	359.00

Interest Rate: 3.9%

Amount you can finance:	Monthly payment amount for:			
	24 months	36 months	48 months	60 months
$ 6,000.00	$ 261.00	$ 177.00	$ 136.00	$ 111.00
6,500.00	282.00	192.00	147.00	120.00
7,000.00	304.00	207.00	158.00	129.00
7,500.00	326.00	222.00	170.00	138.00
8,000.00	348.00	236.00	181.00	147.00
8,500.00	369.00	251.00	192.00	157.00
9,000.00	391.00	266.00	203.00	166.00
9,500.00	413.00	281.00	215.00	175.00
10,000.00	434.00	295.00	226.00	184.00
10,500.00	456.00	310.00	237.00	193.00
11,000.00	478.00	325.00	248.00	203.00
11,500.00	499.00	340.00	260.00	212.00
12,000.00	521.00	354.00	271.00	221.00
12,500.00	543.00	369.00	282.00	230.00
13,000.00	564.00	384.00	293.00	239.00
13,500.00	586.00	398.00	305.00	249.00
14,000.00	608.00	413.00	316.00	258.00
14,500.00	630.00	428.00	327.00	267.00
15,000.00	651.00	443.00	339.00	276.00
15,500.00	673.00	457.00	350.00	285.00
16,000.00	695.00	472.00	361.00	294.00
16,500.00	716.00	487.00	372.00	304.00
17,000.00	738.00	502.00	384.00	313.00
17,500.00	760.00	516.00	395.00	322.00
18,000.00	781.00	531.00	406.00	331.00
18,500.00	803.00	546.00	417.00	340.00
19,000.00	825.00	561.00	429.00	350.00
19,500.00	846.00	575.00	440.00	359.00
20,000.00	868.00	590.00	451.00	368.00

Interest Rate: 4.9%

Amount you can finance:	Monthly payment amount for:			
	24 months	36 months	48 months	60 months
$ 6,000.00	$ 263.00	$ 180.00	$ 138.00	$ 113.00
6,500.00	285.00	195.00	150.00	123.00
7,000.00	307.00	210.00	161.00	132.00
7,500.00	329.00	225.00	173.00	142.00
8,000.00	351.00	240.00	184.00	151.00
8,500.00	373.00	255.00	196.00	161.00
9,000.00	395.00	270.00	207.00	170.00
9,500.00	417.00	285.00	219.00	179.00
10,000.00	439.00	300.00	230.00	189.00
10,500.00	461.00	315.00	242.00	198.00
11,000.00	483.00	330.00	253.00	208.00
11,500.00	505.00	345.00	265.00	217.00
12,000.00	526.00	360.00	276.00	226.00
12,500.00	548.00	375.00	288.00	236.00
13,000.00	570.00	390.00	299.00	245.00
13,500.00	592.00	404.00	311.00	255.00
14,000.00	614.00	419.00	322.00	264.00
14,500.00	636.00	434.00	334.00	273.00
15,000.00	658.00	449.00	345.00	283.00
15,500.00	680.00	464.00	357.00	292.00
16,000.00	702.00	479.00	368.00	302.00
16,500.00	724.00	494.00	380.00	311.00
17,000.00	746.00	509.00	391.00	321.00
17,500.00	767.00	524.00	403.00	330.00
18,000.00	789.00	539.00	414.00	339.00
18,500.00	811.00	554.00	426.00	349.00
19,000.00	833.00	569.00	437.00	358.00
19,500.00	855.00	584.00	449.00	368.00
20,000.00	877.00	599.00	460.00	377.00

Interest Rate: 5.9%

Amount you can finance:	Monthly payment amount for:			
	24 months	36 months	48 months	60 months
$ 6,000.00	$ 266.00	$ 183.00	$ 141.00	$ 116.00
6,500.00	288.00	198.00	153.00	126.00
7,000.00	310.00	213.00	165.00	135.00
7,500.00	333.00	228.00	176.00	145.00
8,000.00	355.00	244.00	188.00	155.00
8,500.00	377.00	259.00	200.00	164.00
9,000.00	399.00	274.00	211.00	174.00
9,500.00	421.00	289.00	223.00	184.00
10,000.00	443.00	304.00	235.00	193.00
10,500.00	465.00	319.00	247.00	203.00
11,000.00	488.00	335.00	258.00	213.00
11,500.00	510.00	350.00	270.00	222.00
12,000.00	532.00	365.00	282.00	232.00
12,500.00	554.00	380.00	293.00	242.00
13,000.00	576.00	395.00	305.00	251.00
13,500.00	598.00	411.00	317.00	261.00
14,000.00	617.00	426.00	329.00	271.00
14,500.00	643.00	441.00	340.00	280.00
15,000.00	665.00	456.00	352.00	290.00
15,500.00	689.00	471.00	364.00	299.00
16,000.00	709.00	487.00	376.00	309.00
16,500.00	731.00	502.00	387.00	319.00
17,000.00	753.00	517.00	399.00	328.00
17,500.00	775.00	532.00	411.00	338.00
18,000.00	797.00	547.00	422.00	348.00
18,500.00	820.00	562.00	434.00	357.00
19,000.00	842.00	578.00	446.00	367.00
19,500.00	864.00	593.00	458.00	377.00
20,000.00	886.00	608.00	469.00	386.00

115

Interest Rate: 6.9%

Amount you can finance:	Monthly payment amount for:			
	24 months	36 months	48 months	60 months
$ 6,000.00	$ 269.00	$ 185.00	$ 144.00	$ 119.00
6,500.00	291.00	201.00	156.00	129.00
7,000.00	314.00	216.00	168.00	139.00
7,500.00	336.00	232.00	180.00	149.00
8,000.00	358.00	247.00	192.00	159.00
8,500.00	381.00	263.00	204.00	168.00
9,000.00	403.00	278.00	216.00	178.00
9,500.00	425.00	293.00	228.00	188.00
10,000.00	448.00	309.00	239.00	198.00
10,500.00	470.00	324.00	251.00	208.00
11,000.00	492.00	340.00	263.00	218.00
11,500.00	515.00	355.00	275.00	228.00
12,000.00	537.00	370.00	287.00	238.00
12,500.00	560.00	386.00	299.00	247.00
13,000.00	582.00	401.00	311.00	257.00
13,500.00	604.00	417.00	323.00	267.00
14,000.00	627.00	432.00	335.00	277.00
14,500.00	649.00	448.00	347.00	287.00
15,000.00	671.00	463.00	359.00	297.00
15,500.00	694.00	478.00	371.00	307.00
16,000.00	716.00	494.00	383.00	317.00
16,500.00	738.00	509.00	395.00	326.00
17,000.00	761.00	525.00	407.00	336.00
17,500.00	783.00	540.00	419.00	346.00
18,000.00	806.00	555.00	431.00	356.00
18,500.00	828.00	571.00	443.00	366.00
19,000.00	850.00	586.00	455.00	376.00
19,500.00	873.00	602.00	467.00	386.00
20,000.00	895.00	617.00	478.00	396.00

Interest Rate: 7.9%

Amount you can finance:	Monthly payment amount for:			
	24 months	36 months	48 months	60 months
$ 6,000.00	$ 272.00	$ 188.00	$ 147.00	$ 122.00
6,500.00	294.00	204.00	159.00	132.00
7,000.00	317.00	220.00	171.00	142.00
7,500.00	339.00	235.00	183.00	152.00
8,000.00	362.00	251.00	195.00	162.00
8,500.00	385.00	266.00	208.00	172.00
9,000.00	407.00	282.00	220.00	183.00
9,500.00	430.00	298.00	232.00	193.00
10,000.00	452.00	313.00	244.00	203.00
10,500.00	475.00	329.00	256.00	213.00
11,000.00	498.00	345.00	269.00	223.00
11,500.00	520.00	360.00	281.00	233.00
12,000.00	543.00	376.00	293.00	243.00
12,500.00	565.00	392.00	305.00	253.00
13,000.00	588.00	407.00	317.00	263.00
13,500.00	610.00	423.00	329.00	274.00
14,000.00	633.00	439.00	342.00	284.00
14,500.00	656.00	454.00	354.00	294.00
15,000.00	678.00	470.00	366.00	304.00
15,500.00	701.00	486.00	378.00	314.00
16,000.00	723.00	501.00	390.00	324.00
16,500.00	746.00	517.00	403.00	334.00
17,000.00	769.00	532.00	415.00	344.00
17,500.00	791.00	548.00	427.00	355.00
18,000.00	814.00	564.00	439.00	365.00
18,500.00	836.00	579.00	451.00	375.00
19,000.00	859.00	595.00	463.00	385.00
19,500.00	882.00	611.00	476.00	395.00
20,000.00	904.00	626.00	488.00	405.00

Interest Rate: 8.9%

Amount you can finance:	Monthly payment amount for: 24 months	36 months	48 months	60 months
$ 6,000.00	$ 274.00	$ 191.00	$ 150.00	$ 125.00
6,500.00	297.00	207.00	162.00	135.00
7,000.00	320.00	223.00	174.00	145.00
7,500.00	343.00	239.00	187.00	156.00
8,000.00	366.00	255.00	199.00	166.00
8,500.00	388.00	270.00	212.00	177.00
9,000.00	411.00	286.00	224.00	187.00
9,500.00	434.00	302.00	236.00	197.00
10,000.00	457.00	318.00	249.00	208.00
10,500.00	480.00	334.00	261.00	218.00
11,000.00	503.00	350.00	274.00	228.00
11,500.00	525.00	366.00	286.00	239.00
12,000.00	548.00	382.00	299.00	249.00
12,500.00	571.00	397.00	311.00	259.00
13,000.00	594.00	413.00	323.00	270.00
13,500.00	617.00	429.00	336.00	280.00
14,000.00	639.00	445.00	348.00	290.00
14,500.00	662.00	461.00	361.00	301.00
15,000.00	685.00	477.00	373.00	311.00
15,500.00	708.00	493.00	385.00	321.00
16,000.00	731.00	509.00	398.00	332.00
16,500.00	754.00	524.00	410.00	342.00
17,000.00	776.00	540.00	423.00	353.00
17,500.00	799.00	556.00	435.00	363.00
18,000.00	822.00	572.00	448.00	373.00
18,500.00	845.00	588.00	460.00	384.00
19,000.00	868.00	604.00	472.00	394.00
19,500.00	890.00	620.00	485.00	404.00
20,000.00	913.00	636.00	497.00	415.00

Interest Rate: 9.9%

Amount you can finance:	Monthly payment amount for:			
	24 months	36 months	48 months	60 months
$ 6,000.00	$ 277.00	$ 194.00	$ 152.00	$ 128.00
6,500.00	300.00	210.00	165.00	138.00
7,000.00	323.00	226.00	178.00	149.00
7,500.00	346.00	242.00	190.00	159.00
8,000.00	369.00	258.00	203.00	170.00
8,500.00	392.00	274.00	216.00	181.00
9,000.00	415.00	290.00	228.00	191.00
9,500.00	438.00	307.00	241.00	202.00
10,000.00	461.00	323.00	254.00	212.00
10,500.00	485.00	339.00	266.00	223.00
11,000.00	508.00	355.00	279.00	234.00
11,500.00	531.00	371.00	292.00	244.00
12,000.00	554.00	387.00	304.00	255.00
12,500.00	577.00	403.00	317.00	265.00
13,000.00	600.00	419.00	330.00	276.00
13,500.00	623.00	435.00	342.00	287.00
14,000.00	646.00	452.00	355.00	297.00
14,500.00	669.00	468.00	368.00	308.00
15,000.00	692.00	484.00	380.00	317.00
15,500.00	715.00	500.00	393.00	329.00
16,000.00	738.00	516.00	406.00	340.00
16,500.00	761.00	532.00	418.00	350.00
17,000.00	784.00	548.00	431.00	361.00
17,500.00	809.00	564.00	444.00	371.00
18,000.00	830.00	580.00	456.00	382.00
18,500.00	853.00	597.00	467.00	393.00
19,000.00	876.00	613.00	481.00	403.00
19,500.00	899.00	629.00	494.00	414.00
20,000.00	922.00	645.00	507.00	424.00

Interest Rate: 10.9%

Amount you can finance:	Monthly payment amount for:			
	24 months	36 months	48 months	60 months
$ 6,000.00	$ 280.00	$ 197.00	$ 155.00	$ 131.00
6,500.00	303.00	213.00	168.00	141.00
7,000.00	326.00	229.00	181.00	152.00
7,500.00	350.00	246.00	194.00	163.00
8,000.00	373.00	262.00	207.00	174.00
8,500.00	396.00	278.00	220.00	185.00
9,000.00	420.00	295.00	233.00	196.00
9,500.00	443.00	311.00	246.00	207.00
10,000.00	466.00	327.00	258.00	217.00
10,500.00	489.00	344.00	271.00	228.00
11,000.00	513.00	360.00	284.00	239.00
11,500.00	536.00	376.00	297.00	250.00
12,000.00	559.00	393.00	310.00	261.00
12,500.00	583.00	409.00	323.00	272.00
13,000.00	606.00	425.00	336.00	282.00
13,500.00	629.00	442.00	349.00	293.00
14,000.00	652.00	458.00	362.00	304.00
14,500.00	676.00	475.00	375.00	315.00
15,000.00	699.00	491.00	387.00	326.00
15,500.00	722.00	507.00	400.00	337.00
16,000.00	745.00	524.00	413.00	348.00
16,500.00	769.00	540.00	426.00	358.00
17,000.00	792.00	556.00	439.00	369.00
17,500.00	815.00	573.00	452.00	380.00
18,000.00	839.00	589.00	465.00	391.00
18,500.00	862.00	605.00	478.00	402.00
19,000.00	885.00	622.00	491.00	413.00
19,500.00	910.00	638.00	504.00	424.00
20,000.00	932.00	654.00	516.00	434.00

Interest Rate: 11.9%

Amount you can finance:	Monthly payment amount for:			
	24 months	36 months	48 months	60 months
$ 6,000.00	$ 283.00	$ 200.00	$ 158.00	$ 134.00
6,500.00	306.00	216.00	171.00	145.00
7,000.00	330.00	233.00	184.00	156.00
7,500.00	353.00	249.00	198.00	167.00
8,000.00	377.00	266.00	211.00	178.00
8,500.00	400.00	282.00	224.00	189.00
9,000.00	424.00	299.00	237.00	200.00
9,500.00	447.00	316.00	250.00	211.00
10,000.00	471.00	332.00	263.00	222.00
10,500.00	494.00	349.00	276.00	234.00
11,000.00	518.00	365.00	290.00	245.00
11,500.00	541.00	382.00	303.00	256.00
12,000.00	565.00	399.00	316.00	267.00
12,500.00	588.00	415.00	329.00	278.00
13,000.00	612.00	432.00	342.00	289.00
13,500.00	635.00	448.00	355.00	300.00
14,000.00	659.00	465.00	368.00	311.00
14,500.00	682.00	481.00	382.00	322.00
15,000.00	706.00	498.00	395.00	333.00
15,500.00	729.00	515.00	408.00	345.00
16,000.00	753.00	531.00	421.00	356.00
16,500.00	776.00	547.00	434.00	367.00
17,000.00	800.00	564.00	447.00	378.00
17,500.00	823.00	581.00	460.00	389.00
18,000.00	847.00	598.00	474.00	400.00
18,500.00	871.00	614.00	487.00	411.00
19,000,00	894.00	631.00	500.00	422.00
19,500.00	918.00	647.00	513.00	433.00
20,000.00	941.00	664.00	526.00	444.00

Interest Rate: 12.9%

Amount you can finance:	Monthly payment amount for:			
	24 months	36 months	48 months	60 months
$ 6,000.00	$ 285.00	$ 202.00	$ 161.00	$ 137.00
6,500.00	309.00	219.00	175.00	148.00
7,000.00	333.00	236.00	188.00	159.00
7,500.00	357.00	253.00	201.00	171.00
8,000.00	380.00	270.00	215.00	182.00
8,500.00	404.00	286.00	228.00	193.00
9,000.00	428.00	303.00	241.00	205.00
9,500.00	452.00	320.00	255.00	216.00
10,000.00	475.00	337.00	268.00	228.00
10,500.00	499.00	354.00	282.00	239.00
11,000.00	523.00	371.00	295.00	250.00
11,500.00	547.00	387.00	308.00	262.00
12,000.00	570.00	404.00	322.00	273.00
12,500.00	594.00	421.00	335.00	284.00
13,000.00	618.00	438.00	349.00	296.00
13,500.00	642.00	455.00	362.00	307.00
14,000.00	665.00	472.00	375.00	318.00
14,500.00	689.00	488.00	389.00	330.00
15,000.00	713.00	505.00	402.00	341.00
15,500.00	737.00	522.00	416.00	352.00
16,000.00	760.00	539.00	429.00	364.00
16,500.00	784.00	556.00	442.00	375.00
17,000.00	809.00	572.00	456.00	386.00
17,500.00	832.00	589.00	469.00	398.00
18,000.00	855.00	606.00	482.00	409.00
18,500.00	879.00	623.00	496.00	420.00
19,000.00	903.00	640.00	509.00	432.00
19,500.00	927.00	657.00	523.00	443.00
20,000.00	950.00	673.00	536.00	455.00

Interest Rate: 13.9%

Amount you can finance:	Monthly payment amount for:			
	24 months	36 months	48 months	60 months
$ 6,000.00	$ 288.00	$ 205.00	$ 164.00	$ 140.00
6,500.00	312.00	222.00	178.00	151.00
7,000.00	336.00	239.00	191.00	163.00
7,500.00	360.00	256.00	205.00	175.00
8,000.00	384.00	274.00	219.00	186.00
8,500.00	408.00	291.00	232.00	198.00
9,000.00	432.00	308.00	246.00	209.00
9,500.00	456.00	325.00	260.00	221.00
10,000.00	480.00	342.00	273.00	233.00
10,500.00	504.00	359.00	287.00	244.00
11,000.00	528.00	376.00	301.00	256.00
11,500.00	552.00	393.00	314.00	267.00
12,000.00	576.00	410.00	328.00	279.00
12,500.00	600.00	427.00	341.00	291.00
13,000.00	624.00	444.00	355.00	302.00
13,500.00	648.00	461.00	369.00	314.00
14,000.00	672.00	478.00	382.00	326.00
14,500.00	696.00	495.00	396.00	337.00
15,000.00	720.00	512.00	410.00	349.00
15,500.00	744.00	530.00	423.00	360.00
16,000.00	768.00	547.00	437.00	372.00
16,500.00	792.00	564.00	451.00	384.00
17,000.00	816.00	581.00	464.00	395.00
17,500.00	840.00	598.00	478.00	407.00
18,000.00	864.00	615.00	491.00	418.00
18,500.00	888.00	632.00	505.00	430.00
19,000.00	912.00	649.00	519.00	442.00
19,500.00	936.00	666.00	532.00	453.00
20,000.00	960.00	683.00	546.00	465.00

Interest Rate: 14.9%

Amount you can finance:	Monthly payment amount for:			
	24 months	36 months	48 months	60 months
$ 6,000.00	$ 291.00	$ 208.00	$ 167.00	$ 143.00
6,500.00	315.00	226.00	181.00	155.00
7,000.00	340.00	243.00	195.00	167.00
7,500.00	364.00	260.00	209.00	179.00
8,000.00	388.00	277.00	223.00	190.00
8,500.00	412.00	295.00	237.00	202.00
9,000.00	436.00	312.00	251.00	214.00
9,500.00	461.00	329.00	264.00	226.00
10,000.00	485.00	347.00	278.00	238.00
10,500.00	509.00	364.00	292.00	250.00
11,000.00	533.00	381.00	306.00	262.00
11,500.00	558.00	399.00	320.00	273.00
12,000.00	582.00	416.00	334.00	285.00
12,500.00	606.00	433.00	348.00	297.00
13,000.00	630.00	451.00	362.00	309.00
13,500.00	654.00	468.00	376.00	321.00
14,000.00	679.00	485.00	389.00	333.00
14,500.00	703.00	502.00	403.00	345.00
15,000.00	727.00	520.00	417.00	357.00
15,500.00	751.00	537.00	431.00	368.00
16,000.00	776.00	554.00	445.00	380.00
16,500.00	800.00	572.00	459.00	392.00
17,000.00	824.00	589.00	473.00	404.00
17,500.00	848.00	606.00	487.00	416.00
18,000.00	872.00	624.00	501.00	428.00
18,500.00	897.00	641.00	514.00	440.00
19,000.00	921.00	658.00	528.00	452.00
19,500.00	945.00	676.00	542.00	463.00
20,000.00	969.00	693.00	556.00	475.00

Interest Rate: 15.9%

Amount you can finance:	Monthly payment amount for:			
	24 months	36 months	48 months	60 months
$ 6,000.00	$ 294.00	$ 211.00	$ 170.00	$ 146.00
6,500.00	318.00	229.00	184.00	158.00
7,000.00	343.00	246.00	199.00	170.00
7,500.00	367.00	264.00	213.00	182.00
8,000.00	392.00	281.00	227.00	195.00
8,500.00	416.00	299.00	241.00	207.00
9,000.00	441.00	316.00	255.00	219.00
9,500.00	465.00	334.00	269.00	231.00
10,000.00	490.00	352.00	283.00	243.00
10,500.00	514.00	369.00	298.00	255.00
11,000.00	539.00	387.00	312.00	267.00
11,500.00	563.00	404.00	326.00	280.00
12,000.00	587.00	422.00	340.00	292.00
12,500.00	612.00	439.00	354.00	304.00
13,000.00	636.00	457.00	368.00	316.00
13,500.00	661.00	474.00	382.00	328.00
14,000.00	685.00	492.00	397.00	340.00
14,500.00	710.00	510.00	411.00	352.00
15,000.00	734.00	527.00	425.00	364.00
15,500.00	759.00	545.00	439.00	377.00
16,000.00	783.00	562.00	453.00	389.00
16,500.00	808.00	580.00	467.00	401.00
17,000.00	832.00	597.00	481.00	413.00
17,500.00	857.00	615.00	495.00	425.00
18,000.00	881.00	632.00	510.00	437.00
18,500.00	905.00	650.00	524.00	449.00
19,000.00	930.00	668.00	538.00	462.00
19,500.00	954.00	685.00	552.00	475.00
20,000.00	979.00	703.00	566.00	486.00

125

Interest Rate: 16.9%

Amount you can finance:	Monthly payment amount for:			
	24 months	36 months	48 months	60 months
$ 6,000.00	$ 297.00	$ 214.00	$ 173.00	$ 149.00
6,500.00	322.00	232.00	188.00	162.00
7,000.00	346.00	250.00	202.00	174.00
7,500.00	371.00	268.00	217.00	186.00
8,000.00	396.00	285.00	231.00	199.00
8,500.00	420.00	303.00	245.00	211.00
9,000.00	445.00	321.00	260.00	224.00
9,500.00	470.00	339.00	274.00	236.00
10,000.00	494.00	357.00	289.00	248.00
10,500.00	519.00	374.00	303.00	261.00
11,000.00	544.00	392.00	317.00	273.00
11,500.00	569.00	410.00	332.00	286.00
12,000.00	596.00	428.00	346.00	298.00
12,500.00	618.00	446.00	361.00	310.00
13,000.00	643.00	463.00	375.00	323.00
13,500.00	667.00	481.00	389.00	335.00
14,000.00	692.00	499.00	404.00	348.00
14,500.00	717.00	517.00	418.00	360.00
15,000.00	741.00	535.00	433.00	372.00
15,500.00	765.00	552.00	447.00	385.00
16,000.00	791.00	570.00	461.00	397.00
16,500.00	815.00	588.00	476.00	410.00
17,000.00	840.00	606.00	490.00	422.00
17,500.00	865.00	624.00	505.00	434.00
18,000.00	890.00	641.00	519.00	447.00
18,500.00	914.00	659.00	533.00	459.00
19,000.00	939.00	677.00	548.00	472.00
19,500.00	964.00	695.00	562.00	484.00
20,000.00	988.00	713.00	577.00	496.00

Plan-of-Action Workbook

Plan-of-Action Checklist

1. I have completed my Disposable Income Budget Form. _____
2. My monthly-payment budget is $_____
3. I have completed my Needs Inventory Checklist _____
4. I have completed by "Out-the-Door" Price Worksheet. _____
5. I have completed my "Out-the-Door" Cost Worksheet. _____
6. My trade-in appraisals:

        Dealer A $_____

        Dealer B. $_____

        Dealer C $_____

7. I have **two** prequalified loans at:

    A:_____% Interest   B:_____% Interest

8. Dealer invoice on the cars I am considering:

    A: Car_____ $ _____

    B: Car_____ $ _____

    C: Car_____ $ _____

    D: Car_____ $ _____

9. I am going to shop the following dealerships:

    A: _____

    B: _____

    C: _____

    D: _____

    E: _____

Notes:_____

_____

_____

Disposable Income Budget Form

Monthly take-home pay $ _____

Deduct the following monthly expenses:

Mortgage/Rent   _____

Gas/Electric   _____

Telephone   _____

Groceries   _____

Life/Health insurance   _____

Auto insurance*   _____

Car payment**   _____

Gasoline   _____

Major credit cards   _____

Other charge cards   _____

Personal loans   _____

Unexpected expenses***   _____

Entertainment   _____

Disposable income $ _____

   *Auto insurance figure will change.
**If you will be trading in your car do not include this figure.

      After deducting all monthly expenses, your disposable income is what remains to meet any new financial obligations.

Needs Inventory Checklist

I am considering buying:

Car _____ Truck _____ Mini-van _____

Other _____

I need:

2 doors _____ 4 doors _____ Other _____

I need:

Automatic transmission _____ Manual transmission _____

What I dislike about my current car:

_____

_____

_____

What I like about my current car:

_____

_____

_____

Repair problems I have with my current car:

_____

_____

_____

Options I should have purchased on my last car:

_____

_____

_____

Options I should not have purchased on my last car:

_____

_____

_____

Out-the-Door Price Worksheet

Monthly payment budget .... $ _____

Interest rate qualified for .... _____%

Turn to the Interest-Rate chart for your qualified rate and find the amount you can finance for each of the payment terms. Fill them in below.

Amount you can finance for:

24 months .... $ _____

36 months .... $ _____

48 months .... $ _____

60 months .... $ _____

Using each of the above amounts, determine your out-the-door new-car budget as follows:

Cash down payment available $ _____

Wholesale trade-in value $ _____

Amount You Can Finance $ _____

Out-the-Door $ _____*

*Each term will give you a different out-the-door total.

Example:

Payment Budget (approx) $ _____ 300.00

Interest Rate Qualified for   _____ 11.9%

Amount you can finance for:

24 months .... $ _____ 6,500.00

36 months .... $ _____ 9,000.00

48 months .... $ _____ 11,500.00

60 months .... $ _____ 13,500.00

Cash down payment available $ _____ 2,500.00

Wholesale trade-in value $ _____ 2,200.00

Amount you can finance

(Term selected: 48 months) $ _____ 11,500.00

Your out-the-door budget $ 16,200.00*

*This is the total amount you can spend for your new car without raising your payments. (Total includes tax, license, and documentary fee.)

Out-the-Door Cost Worksheet

Dealer invoice .... $ _____

Profit to dealer .... $ _____

Less rebates (if applicable) .... $ _____

Less dealer incentive
(if applicable) .... $ _____

Total sale price .... $ _____

Local sales tax at __ % .... $ _____

State license fee .... $ _____

Estimated documentary fee
(if applicable) .... $ _____

Total out-the-door cost .... $ _____*

*This figure *cannot* exceed your Out-the-door Budget without affecting your budgeted monthly payment.

Example

Dealer invoice .... $ 16,897.50

Profit to dealer .... $ +   300.00

Less rebates (if applicable) .... $ − 1,800.00

Less dealer incentive
(if applicable) .... $ 0.00

Total sale price .... $ 15,397.50

Local sales tax at 6.0% .... $ 923.85*

State license fee .... $ 350.00*

Estimated documentary fee
(if applicable) .... $ 0.00

Total out-the-door cost .... $ **16,771.35***

*The sales tax and license fees in your state may be different from those in the example. Be sure to use the correct figures.

Car Evaluation Checklist

If you are buying a used car, this worksheet will help you determine possible costs in order to get that car into good condition. If you are buying a new car, this checklist will help you make sure that everything is as it should be before you take delivery. Follow it closely and see how many flaws you can find in your new car.

Fill out this form **completely** if you want a realistic evaluation. Each category will rate the car either a 1, a 3, or a 5. A 1 indicates poor condition, a 3 indicates average condition, and a 5 indicates excellent condition.

Add the total number of 1s, 3s and 5s. If you have mostly 1s, the car is not in very good condition. If you have mostly 3s, you are looking at an average car. If you have mostly 5s, consider yourself lucky because you are looking at a car that is in top condition.

Year _____ Make _____

Model _____

Trim level (LS, XLT, SE Limited, etc.) _____

Body style: 2-Door ( ) 4-Door ( ) Convertible ( )

Station wagon ( ) Hatchback ( ) Van ( ) Pickup ( )

2-Wheel Drive ( ) 4-Wheel Drive ( ) All-Wheel Drive ( )

Engine type _____

Engine size _____

Transmission type _____

Vehicle ID number* _____

*(ID # is important for proper "blue book" pricing)

Condition Checklist

(Select 1, 3, or 5)

Exterior:

Dents in body : 1 3 5
Paint: 1 3 5
Signs of Plastic Body Filler: 1 3 5
Window glass: 1 3 5
Vinyl top: 1 3 5
Convertible top: 1 3 5
Chrome trim: 1 3 5
Front bumper: 1 3 5
Wiper blades: 1 3 5
Window rubber: 1 3 5
Radio antenna: 1 3 5
Outside mirrors: 1 3 5
Door handles and locks: 1 3 5
Gas cap: 1 3 5
Rear Bumper: 1 3 5
Grill: 1 3 5
Headlight and turn signal/Park lights: 1 3 5
Taillights/Brake lights/Rear park lights: 1 3 5
Wheels or hubcaps: 1 3 5
Tires: 1 3 5
Exhaust system: 1 3 5
Front suspension: 1 3 5
Oil spots under car: 1 3 5

Running/Driving Condition:

Ease of starting: 1 3 5
Engine cold idle speed: 1 3 5
Engine warm idle speed: 1 3 5
Vibration in steering wheel when idling: 1 3 5
Engine revs up and down smoothly: 1 3 5
Quietness of exhaust system: 1 3 5
Smoke from exhaust system: 1 3 5

If automatic transmission:
    Smoothness of shifting from park into drive: 1 3 5
    Smoothness of acceleration: 1 3 5
    Smoothness of shifting: 1 3 5
If manual transmission:
    Smoothness of clutch releasing from dead stop: 1 3 5
    Smoothness of shifting while moving: 1 3 5
Car's ability to track straight: 1 3 5
Brake's ability to stop straight: 1 3 5
Brake squeal: 1 3 5
Brake grinding noise: 1 3 5
Brake pedal travel: 1 3 5
Brake pulsation: 1 3 5

Engine compartment:
Engine cleanliness: 1 3 5
Fluid levels: 1 3 5
Battery hold-down: 1 3 5
Air filter: 1 3 5
Radiator hoses: 1 3 5
Heater hoses: 1 3 5
Fan belts: 1 3 5
Vacuum lines: 1 3 5
Radiator: 1 3 5
Smog equipment: 1 3 5
Hood support (if applicable): 1 3 5
Windshield washer reservoir: 1 3 5
Plug wires all match: 1 3 5

Trunk compartment:
Trunk carpeting (if applicable): 1 3 5
Rubber trunk mat (if applicable): 1 3 5
Spare tire: 1 3 5
Properly inflated: 1 3 5
Jack complete and working: 1 3 5

Interior

Seat belt function: 1 3 5
Seat back releases (if applicable): 1 3 5
Seat adjusters (manual): 1 3 5
Seat adjusters (power): 1 3 5
Seat recliners: 1 3 5
Headrests: 1 3 5
Door panels: 1 3 5
Door handles: 1 3 5
Window cranks (manual): 1 3 5
Windows (power): 1 3 5
Door locks (power): 1 3 5
Door locks (manual): 1 3 5
Interior dome light: 1 3 5
Rear-view mirror: 1 3 5
Visors: 1 3 5
Sunroof (if applicable): 1 3 5
Upholstery condition (tears, fading, burns): 1 3 5
Armrests: 1 3 5
Dash top: 1 3 5
Carpeting: 1 3 5
Floor mats: 1 3 5
Sound system: 1 3 5
Speakers: 1 3 5
Instruments: 1 3 5
Headlights: 1 3 5
Air-conditioning system: 1 3 5
Heater/Ventilation: 1 3 5
Defrosters: 1 3 5
Turn signals: 1 3 5
Horn: 1 3 5
Tilt wheel: 1 3 5
Cruise control: 1 3 5
Windshield wipers: 1 3 5
Washers: 1 3 5

Rear defroster: 1 3 5
Rear wiper/Washer: 1 3 5
Glove compartment: 1 3 5
Lighter: 1 3 5
Headliner: 1 3 5
Emergency Flashers: 1 3 5

Total number of 1s circled: _____

Total number of 3s circled: _____

Total number of 5s circled: _____

Majority of 1s indicates a car in poor condition.
Majority of 3s indicates a car in average condition.
Majority of 5s indicates a car in excellent condition.

This worksheet works *only* if you evaluate honestly and fairly. If you do any less, you are fooling yourself.

Bill of Sale

I, _____, for value received in the amount of
$ _____ , do hereby sell and convey to
_____ the following described vehicle:
_____ _____ _____ _____

    I further state that I am the sole legal owner of the above described vehicle and further state that said vehicle meets all applicable federal and state safety and emission requirements that were in effect when vehicle was manufactured, and that such equipment is fully functional as intended.

    I further warrant that all State Department of Motor Vehicle license and registration fees are current and that there are no outstanding citations or violations for which the buyer may be compelled to pay penalties.

    I further indicate the following as an enticement for buyer to purchase said vehicle: _____
_____
_____
_____

    I make no other claims either verbally or in writing as to the condition of the car. Buyer has had the opportunity to examine and drive said car and further has been given the opportunity to have the car examined by an independent facility at (his/her) own expense. Buyer is satisfied with the claims stated above and understands that no other claims have been made except those stated above. I understand that I can and will be held liable for the statements made in this document. I further agree that, should legal action be required to enforce such claims, I, the seller, shall be liable for any and all court costs incurred.

Dated this _____ day of _____ , 19 _____

Seller: _____

Buyer: _____

Witness or Notary: _____

Dealership Paperwork Checklist

_____ **Double check vehicle identification number**

_____ Finance contract and/or purchase agreement

_____ Promissory note for deferred payment (if applicable)

_____ State Department of Motor Vehicle documents
(or copies for your records)

_____ Power of Attorney (copy for your records)

_____ Warranty Registration Book, properly filled out

_____ Extended Warranty Registration, filled out and checked

_____ Federal Warranty Notification Sticker (if a used car)

_____ Promissory note or Due bill from dealer, filled out and
signed by dealership manager

_____ Customer Satisfaction Questionnaire

_____ Smog and/or Safety Inspection Certificate (if applicable)

You should receive a copy of everything you sign.
Insist on it!

Private-Party Paperwork Checklist

_____ Copy of advertisement for vehicle

_____ **Double check vehicle identification number**

_____ Copy of Bill of Sale

_____ Clear Proof of Ownership, checked

_____ Proof of *current* registration

_____ Smog and/or Safety Inspection Certificate(s)

_____ Receipts and/or proof of warranty for any transferable
warranty items